THE
INDISPENSABLE
ACADEMIC LIBRARIAN

THE INDISPENSABLE ACADEMIC LIBRARIAN

Teaching and Collaborating for Change

MICHELLE REALE

ALA
Editions
CHICAGO   2018

MICHELLE REALE an associate professor at Arcadia University near Philadelphia, Pennsylvania, is an access services and outreach librarian as well as a fully embedded librarian in two English courses. Reale holds a master's degree in English and an MFA in poetry from Arcadia University and an MSLS from Clarion University of Pennsylvania. She is also the author of *Mentoring and Managing in the Academic Library* (2013), *Becoming an Embedded Librarian: Making Connections in the Classroom* (2015), and *Becoming a Reflective Librarian and Teacher: Strategies for Mindful Academic Practice* (2017).

© 2018 by the American Library Association

Extensive effort has gone into ensuring the reliability of the information in this book; however, the publisher makes no warranty, express or implied, with respect to the material contained herein.

ISBNs:
978-0-8389-1638-4 (paper)
978-0-8389-1710-7 (PDF)
978-0-8389-1709-1 (ePub)
978-0-8389-1711-4 (Kindle)

Library of Congress Cataloging in Publication Control Number: 2018001085

Text design and composition by Dianne M. Rooney using Janson Text and ITC Avant Garde Gothic typefaces.

♾ This paper meets the requirements of ANSI/NISO Z39.48–1992 (Permanence of Paper).

Printed in the United States of America

22 21 20 19 18   5 4 3 2 1

*Thank you to my wonderful parents
who continue to lift and encourage me.
Thank you to Kaylynn Hills for her friendship,
encouragement, and sharp eyes.
I am deeply grateful.*

Contents

Introduction

The professional literature is rife with stories of the many and varied changes in our profession, which have left librarians, in theory and in practice, to limn the line between delivering what I term "beck-and-call service" and seeing ourselves as educators both in and out of the classroom. I have long perceived, and am by no means unique in the feeling, that academic librarians need to fully recognize ourselves not only as collaborators but also as true educators in the learning cycle of our colleges and universities.

Not surprisingly, librarians have often been thought of as teaching mere "skills," an activity seen as a lower-level endeavor than that of a classroom professor who formally teaches and encourages knowledge creation. We are seen as people who merely curate knowledge structures and provide access to those structures. Some might wonder why that is such a bad thing. While I am not saying that it is untrue, this is only a part of what we do. It is a reductionist way of looking at our profession, and is wholly inaccurate as well. Every day, librarians initiate and encourage learning in both structured and unstructured areas. Not many would think of the work that librarians do across the reference desk as teaching, but that is exactly what it is. Each time a librarian comes in contact with a student, there will likely be potential for learning.

Librarians must also have intentionality when we talk about our contributions to the profession: we have our own theories, our own best practices, our own standards, and our own guidelines. Embracing these empowers us to be proactive in the educational environment and make decisions about our teaching based on what we know from our own studies and research. For instance, this knowledge and confidence enables us to tell a professor that it is a bad idea to schedule a "one-shot" instruction session before an assignment has even been given out, or to suggest another time to instruct a class if we've only been scheduled to fill in when a professor is at a conference or on vacation. We can provide alternatives based on our knowledge. To do this, we must assert our positions, and to do so we need to be secure in our knowledge that what we do is not an add-on, but instead a strong influence on students' future interactions with librarians. Few faculty members would be willing to serve in the same educational capacity that is often required of librarians.

Promotion and tenure can be controversial issues. Although I understand their importance, I will not address these topics because others have already explored them thoroughly. My intention in this volume is to offer a philosophy of librarians as educators and to exemplify the many ways in which librarians are an integral part of teaching. Ultimately, my goal is to clarify our roles and offer ways to strengthen our teaching for students, the faculty with whom we collaborate, and, of course, ourselves.

（1）

Librarians in Academia

A Place at the Table

*The time was when a library was very much like a
museum and a librarian was a mouser in musty books . . .
The time is when a library is a school, and the
librarian is in the highest sense a teacher.*

—MELVIL DEWEY

Those of us in the profession know that librarianship has been changing and continues to evolve rapidly, but those with whom we work and those we serve often do not. Librarianship, perhaps more than any other profession that I can think of, has constantly suffered not only from stereotypes (about which volumes have literally been written), but also from misconceptions about librarians' mission, our very essence, as educators rather than mere auxiliaries to others whose mandates are perceived to be more important. In academic librarianship, these are the professors with whom we work, especially if we work at institutions where we have faculty status. There is a subtle negation of librarians as educators in the real and true sense, which may be based in the not-too-distant past when librarians were seen solely as teachers of "skills" that were considered necessary for research. Although skills are considered valuable on some levels, they are viewed as distinct from "knowledge," perhaps because the skilled trades do not require a formal, higher education. However, although the ways we practice librarianship have changed, the manner in which others, both professors and administrators, perceive us has not. Despite my title, my scholarship, and my ubiquitous presence in the classroom and all over campus, my experiences over the years have confirmed this. I ask myself: do I wish to be more than what I am, indeed, more than what all of us are? I have considered this, particularly after a conversation about teaching with a then-colleague who told me that she didn't become a librarian to stand in front of a classroom, as our new faculty status required. At the time I sympathized with her without thinking through what she was saying. Her implication was that not only did she not want to be an educator, but that she did not *think* of herself as an educator, which troubled me for what I hope are obvious reasons. However, her sentiments did not make me question how I thought of myself as a faculty member or as a faculty librarian. The term *faculty librarian* is in and of itself confusing because it implies that librarians are not *part* of faculty but instead exist solely *for* faculty. And when librarians themselves impose limits on the profession, it only serves to reinforce how we are perceived within the academy.

I then set out on my own quest to explore some recent history and identify what our predecessors thought about our role in academia. I began making my way through old issues of the *Wilson Library Bulletin*, because I've always felt that placing myself within the context of librarianship today entails learning about the profession as it was practiced twenty, thirty, forty, or more years ago. As I began to read back issues, I confirmed what I had always tacitly known, and what has been addressed in the literature from as far back as the early 1900s: that librarianship can be embattled in its perception of itself, but has always gradually and steadily grown and changed. In the past fifteen years much of this has been due to burgeoning technology (particularly the internet), but change had been brewing even before that.

When I stumbled on Mary Graver's 1969 article, "The Librarian in the Academic Community—A New Breed?," I read it with great interest. I was grateful to this trailblazing author for writing so eloquently about librarians in the academy. Graver's article is a clarion call to acknowledge how librarians enrich campuses nationwide and how our efforts—indeed, our mandate—is teaching in all of its many forms. As Graver went on to lament the myriad problems facing academic libraries and the librarians who work in them, she did something very important: she claimed, on behalf of all librarians, a place at the academic table. Perhaps she was not the first to do so, but the articulate way she portrayed not only the realities but also the possibilities of the profession was especially inspiring. Her article gave me a renewed understanding that librarianship is teaching in every sense of the word. In my opinion, when we incessantly argue this point, we undercut our ourselves and undermine our rightful place at the table.[1]

What Graver understood in 1969 was that an opportunity was presenting itself that would change our place in the educational cycle of higher education for the better. In 1969, nearly every bit of the social fabric of life had been ripped and turned inside-out. Education was no exception; it had become a hotbed of protest against an old system. Graver was, in essence, riding that wave. She was not advocating for an exalted position for librarians, as some critics of the librarian-as-faculty like to claim, but rather that we yearn to be more than what we are. Her desire was for partnership within the academy, that "one of the characteristics of the new breed of college librarian—whom we already have some examples of in the profession—then, will be the demand on their part that they be a partner with the faculty."[2]

The word *demand* is an interesting choice, because it is not easily reconciled with the persistent stereotypes that we all know and loathe. But it is the right word. Graver goes on to make the distinction between those members of the library staff who are integral to the smooth running of everyday operations and those who work directly with faculty—those who strive "to develop the spirit of inquiry among all its students—that is, the process of learning and teaching in which information is examined and evaluated." Further, she states that we "will need librarians who themselves are liberally educated, who have strong commitment to concepts of intellectual freedom, and whose professional education has provided the background of and principle by which they are competent to work with the faculty as true partners."[3]

In describing the new breed of librarian in academia, Graver very clearly draws a line between what was and what can, should, and *will be* if she has anything to say about it! It marks a place in time when the winds of change began to stir. In some ways 1969 seems a world away, and yet in 2018 we still debate the issue of whether librarianship is a teaching or a service profession, whether we are teachers or merely teachers' aides.

In 1984, periodicals librarian David Peele wrote the article "Librarians as Teachers: Some Reality, Mostly Myth," which was an impassioned attempt to challenge the existing literature asserting that librarians are teachers. He sought to debunk the myth of the librarian-as-teacher by presenting what he considered to be specific reasons why librarians were not in fact educators. In my humble opinion, this was a strange and wrong-headed approach, and a disservice to the many librarians fighting on the front lines to gain respect for their difficult and integral work. While I could understand some of Peele's points, I did not agree with his game plan. It hurts no one to recognize the work of librarians as teachers; indeed, it only helps to elevate our stature. But to assert the opposite seems pointless, and can be used to validate the reasons why, despite the fact that we do teach, we should be kept in our place—far from any opportunities to influence the students, scholarship, and governance that are the domain of faculty. Sounding for all the world like a reluctant teenager going to Grandma's on Sunday afternoon, Peele finally asks, "Why is it that we desire to be teachers anyway? Why are we not content with the title 'Librarian?' What is it that they have that we don't, but want?"[4]

Why continue to beat what some consider a dead horse? We know that language shapes our perception of reality, and therefore it stands to reason that not only how we *think* of ourselves, but how we *talk* about ourselves *within* the profession, is not only vitally important, but wholly necessary to further shape our work and to become fully accepted for what we are: a vital and necessary force in the greater academic universe. We are, in so many different ways, indispensable.

Graver's article clearly articulated what I had been thinking about this issue and how colleagues and others also felt about it. Interestingly, ours may be one of the few professions that has reluctantly tolerated, but tolerated nonetheless, others' characterizations of us to the point that it has shaped our reality in many ways.

SERVICE DOES NOT MEAN SERVILE

One of the most interesting and fallacious arguments against librarianship as a teaching profession is that it is above all a service profession. As others have asserted, and I too will jump on the bandwagon, it can be argued that *all* professions are service professions—even some of the highest paid! I am happy to say that Graver addresses that issue too: "The emphasis on service, which is a fundamental criterion for any profession, requires that the professional look in two ways: towards service to the client, and individual, and towards the means of that service, the agency or artifact, which is unique to his profession."

Graver goes on to emphasize that in 1969, when the field was just beginning to see the emergence of new media, librarians had a fresh opportunity to provide "service whose integrity is determined by its content, not its format." What this means to me is that books were no longer the primary preoccupation of librarians—as if they ever should have been—but rather that connecting people with information in whatever form is what is required from the new breed of librarian. Through all of this, Graver acknowledges that the battle to be considered a full and equal partner of faculty may be based in different views of scholarship—though one can surmise that ego may have something to do with it as well. Graver is not cowed, not by a long shot, as she goes on to talk about the importance of the new breed of librarian to "evidence a new sense of pride in and responsibility to his own discipline of librarianship, not derogate it as inferior to a subject discipline or as one which is only derivative or whose role is merely subsidiary to the institution to which it serves," which is still true to this day.[5]

The stereotype of librarians has been fodder for writers, comedians, and others who have in part contributed to our difficulty in establishing exactly who and what we are. Librarianship is not a monolith, but even though librarians come in all shapes, sizes, colors, ethnicities, and specialties, we should be able to agree about our basic function. To say that we have experienced, perhaps since our inception, an identity crisis would be stating the obvious. Why that happened is a different question. Although I do not have the answer, I have given it a lot of thought during the time I have been a librarian.

We do not, as a group, define our own identity. It is often defined by others, and perhaps therein lies the problem. Burke, Owens, Serpe, and Thoits assert that identity is, at its very core, "what it means to be who one is." Writing about identity theory, Stryker and Burke propose that while others' expectations of an individual's identity may contribute to the story, they are not the whole story because "individuals define their own identities internally as they accept or reject role expectations as part of who they are." If our professional identities (which are, for all intents and purposes, our "worth") are in conflict, stress will be the direct result as we attempt to satisfy ourselves in our workaday lives and attempt to live up to or surpass the expectations of others.[6]

I have personally experienced this stress. As a newly graduated librarian, I felt eager and empowered—which may be a promising combination in some arenas, but is not always appreciated in academia. I was eager because I'd been working in libraries my whole life before obtaining my MSLS degree, and now that I had it, I was incredibly, incredibly proud of it. For me, libraries were always a place of refuge, a retreat as well as a treat. As a shy high-school girl, I took shelter in the library at lunchtime with our librarian, Sister Consolata Maria, a woman who loved her profession and somehow sensed my loneliness and my affinity for the quiet (she insisted on it!) space. She was an advocate for orderliness at a time when nothing felt right, least of all the way I felt about myself. At the time I envied her education and the fact that she was already a librarian, which was something I wanted to be but thought I'd never achieve.

For many years I held a paraprofessional job in a public library system that was pure bliss, although I'd be lying if I did not admit my envy of the librarians—especially because my fellow paraprofessional staff and I were constantly reminded that we were not professionals. Assuming the mantle of "librarian" became very, very important to me. Not surprisingly, when I did become a librarian and began work at a university, I felt my position was unique, important, and dare I say, exalted. However, others did not. That this came as a shock to me is not easy to admit—I feel foolish writing the words. It is, however, true. Faculty rarely acknowledged me, seldom called on me for my expertise, and had very little insight into what I (or my colleagues) did. Worse, they had very little interest in finding out.

As much as I'd like to admit that I did not care about others' perceptions of me and my work, the fact is that I was greatly affected by it. At least in the beginning, it made me more cautious and tentative than I needed or wanted to be. I felt that there were clearly drawn lines and I was not on the same side as faculty. In fact, at my university librarians were classified not as faculty, but as staff. I valued and deeply honored my profession and my place in it, and it was a rude awakening when I came to understand that others did not. In our lives, we nurture and engage in multiple identities, and, depending on the community in which we move, we let certain characteristics of those identities become more prominent than others.

I had decisions to make. Although I loved my profession and was devoted to it and to those it served, I was very sure that I did not want to spend the majority of my time and effort convincing others of my worth or explaining what it was I actually did. I reasoned that my energy was better spent on students. Lao Tzu famously proclaimed, "the way to do is to be." My interpretation of this helped me to move forward and carry out my work in the best way that I could. Recognition in the academic world in general, and on campus in particular, was less about ego (although I will admit to just a bit of that), and more about a seat at the table. To reach students, in many cases, requires going through the faculty who teach and advise them. It was important to be *seen* as having value in order to have the opportunity to add value, to be able to work with students and fully collaborate with faculty—in other words, to get that seat at the table. Like most academic library environments, mine was changing. With the hiring of a new library director who urged us, in the strongest terms, to call ourselves "faculty librarians," the shift was finally complete. At first slowly, and then at nearly warp speed, we were integrated into nearly all academic departments on campus. We were doing our work steadily, and in my case sometimes shakily, but doing it nonetheless. My own personal commitment to my work increased, and I believe I can assert the same for my colleagues, both past and present. I came to understand that how we think of ourselves—and to some extent how others think of us—has the potential to either limit or expand what is possible to achieve in our profession.[7]

The quotation at the beginning of this chapter is an interesting one. It might seem that in Dewey's time, the issue of librarians' status as teachers was set—that they'd gotten over the hump of the perennial identity crisis and could wear the mantle of "educator." We know this was not true, and this is not even unanimously accepted today. Dewey's assertion may have been premature, but I used the quote because it signaled an ideology, a way of being. And although he clearly jumped the gun, Dewey also had a clear vision for the profession—one that I appreciate and can relate to today. In my own quest to form my own professional identity, I find it crucial to see how long ago the intentionality to recognize librarians as teachers originated.

When we claim a place at the table, it is important to arrive with a strong, professional identity. Claire McGuinness recognizes some popular arguments about "encouraging teaching librarians to think about what their role means." They include:[8]

- confidence
- motivation
- communication with outsiders
- professional identity
- identification of training needs

McGuinness goes on to explain what most of us have, unfortunately, already experienced in the academic environments in which we work: "The teaching experiences of teaching librarians are only partly understood." It is the responsibility of librarians to walk with confidence, to be clear about who we are, to educate others about what we do, and to identify how and when we need extra training, mentoring, or additional educational opportunities to fulfill our own teaching desires, missions, and assignments. In this way, we take responsibility for our own identities and opportunities to expand and grow.[9]

In a study on traditional teachers' identity, Beijaard identifies categories that intersect in building and solidifying an identity:

- the subject being taught

- the teacher's relationship with his or her students
- the role of the teacher and his or her conception of that role[10]

Although this applies to traditional teachers, it can also give librarians an idea of where to focus and reflect, bearing in mind that these aspects of teaching come in addition to our other layers of responsibility. But it is definitely a place to start to build our identities as teachers, and we can fit them in alongside the other aspects of what we do, albeit perhaps a little uncomfortably.

FINAL THOUGHTS

I am fascinated by the novelist Chimamanda Ngozi Adichie's view of "the danger of a single story." In her insightful TED talk, Adichie explicates the dangers of only one story being told from a consistent and mistaken point of view about anyone or anything. This exemplifies the adage "tell a story long enough and people will believe it," despite evidence to the contrary. In many people's minds, only one story about the librarian in academia is still told, even though so many of us have expanded and updated our roles and missions in the academic environment. There are those who would keep us where they want us: fulfilling the outdated and harmful stereotype of the librarian-servant, who is not particularly intellectual, is befuddled by the intricacies of teaching, and is ignorant of pedagogical methods. These stereotypes are harmful largely because many in the profession have internalized them and believe in them. Those who do so will never realize their full potential in the classroom and recognize the absolute necessity for reinvention in a profession that has changed rapidly over time, and continues to do so. [11]

In their excellent article "Exploring the Future of Academic Libraries: A Definitional Approach," Sennyey, Ross, and Mills urge librarians to strive for "more active participation in the scholarly life of the campus." Every profession grows and evolves over time, expanding services to meet the needs of a new paradigm. Those who consistently try to put librarians in a box—especially if they are in the profession—do a disservice to themselves, their colleagues, faculty, and students. We should be assiduous in our efforts to be recognized as integral to the educational process and cycle, careful about the way we talk about what we do, and work hard to collaborate with faculty as colleagues who have common goals. We truly do make the road by walking it![12]

Strategies

- Recognize all the ways librarians are teachers. For instance, Loesch recognizes that "academic librarians transform patron questions into teaching opportunities constantly," an assertion that is foundational in our mission.[13]

- Reject limitations imposed on the profession, whether inside or outside of the library. These stereotypes are powerful, persistent, and ultimately harmful—don't buy into them.

- Relationships are extremely important. Optimize any opportunity to develop them with faculty and others. Placing ourselves among and beside faculty in the classroom and other settings on campus is paramount.

- Develop opportunities within your liaison area(s) to co-teach a class and become the embedded librarian in a research-writing class or a capstone course. Collaboration is integral to the librarian in the academic setting.

- Be confident in your mission. Reflect on your experience. Keep moving forward.

NOTES

1. Mary V. Graver, "The Librarian in the Academic Community—A New Breed?" *Wilson Library Bulletin* (1969).
2. Ibid.
3. Ibid.
4. David Peele, "Librarians as Teachers: Some Reality, Mostly Myth," *Journal of Academic Librarianship* 10, no. 5 (1984): 267–71.
5. Graver, "The Librarian in the Academic Community," 541–43.

6. Peter J. Burke, Timothy J. Owens, Richard T. Serpe, and Peggy A. Thoits, eds., *Advances in Identity Theory and Research* (New York: Kluwer Academic/Plenum Publishers, 2003); Sheldon Stryker and Peter J. Burke, "The Past, Present, and Future of an Identity Theory," *Social Psychology Quarterly* (2000): 284–97; Carol L. Colbeck, "Professional Identity Development Theory and Doctoral Education," *New Directions for Teaching and Learning*, no. 113 (2008): 9–16; Sheldon Stryker, "Identity Salience and Role Performance: The Relevance of Symbolic Interaction Theory for Family Research," *Journal of Marriage and the Family* (1968): 558–64.

7. Lao Tzu, "The Way of Life According to Lao Tzu," trans. Witter Bynner, (New York: Perigee Books, 1944).

8. Claire McGuinness, *Becoming Confident Teachers: A Guide for Academic Librarians*, (Elsevier, 2011).

9. Ibid., 34–35.

10. D. Beijaard, "Teachers' Prior Experiences and Actual Perceptions of Professional Identity," *Teachers and Teaching* 1 (2), 281–94.

11. Chimamanda Adichie, "The Danger of a Single Story" (TED Talk: Ideas Worth Spreading, 2009).

12. Pongracz Sennyey, Lyman Ross, and Caroline Mills, "Exploring the Future of Academic Libraries: A Definitional Approach," *The Journal of Academic Librarianship* 35, no. 3 (2009): 252–59.

13. Martha Fallahay Loesch, "Librarian as Professor: A Dynamic New Role Model," *Education Libraries* 33, no. 1 (2010).

2

Teaching at the Reference Desk

The Reference Librarian, even in the simplest provision
of information, performs the function of teacher.

—JOHN BUDD

One of the most identifiable facets of librarianship, even for those who don't truly know what librarians do (the majority of people!), is the reference desk, staffed by the requisite prune-faced spinster or milquetoast young woman in cat-eye glasses. This image has been immortalized in popular media, where it usually is the only portrayal of librarianship. Few outside of the profession would describe what occurs at that desk as teaching. But it is undeniable that teaching is exactly what occurs there. I know that other things go on at the reference desk (responding to requests to unjam printers, pointing out the restrooms, and fixing staplers), but what I'd like to concentrate on is that reference is a foundational aspect of our work, so much so that it might be said to inform everything else that we do: it is that fundamental.

Most librarians cut their teeth on reference work. Because so many of us have had an affinity for libraries for most of our lives, we also have personal experience approaching a reference desk. I'd worked in the public library system for many years before becoming an academic librarian, and saw the importance of reference librarians, especially to underserved populations. They offered computer help to senior citizens and after-school help to youth who had no computers. As a lifelong library user, I took great comfort in the presence of the reference librarian, with her glasses on a chain and ready smile. Although this was a time when women dressed in skirts or dresses in the workplace, and the profession was considered "ladylike," she would get on the floor with maps, spread a term paper out on a large table, and run down one aisle and up the next gathering resources for a student. I was the recipient of her help several times, although none required such athleticism. I counted on her help and imagined her brilliant children, so lucky to have such a resource at home.

In the academic community, it is not a stretch to say that wherever a student encounters a librarian, teaching, and its byproduct learning, have the potential to happen and usually do. I have been approached in nearly every corner where I can be found on campus—and even approached virtually on Facebook. People identify the process of learning with us, the librarians. I cannot say that I'm always approached at a good time—sometimes it isn't, but I can always arrange to meet at a more convenient time and place. Indeed, it is incumbent that I do, so that the opportunity for learning has half a chance. Granted, some students simply want easy answers, or to plumb the depth of my knowledge on any given topic (often citations!). But that usually isn't the case. When I am asked a question via email, I often will respond with a few emails of my own, something for which students have very little patience. As one frantic student replied: "You answered a question with a question and what I need is an answer. Just tell me where to find it!" Well! Teachable moment!

REFERENCE PEDAGOGY

Elmborg makes a compelling argument for reference services when he asserts that the reference desk "can be a powerful teaching station—more powerful, perhaps, than the classroom." However, he cautions that "if we want to realize this potential, we will need a new framework for understanding reference work—a pedagogy of the reference desk."[1]

Reference work was not initially part of the librarian's mandate; this is yet another way that the profession has grown and changed over the course of more than a century. The main focus of a librarian's job was to acquire and organize materials to allow patrons and students to locate and figure out how to use the information on their own. Samuel Green's "Personal Relations between Librarians and Readers," published in what is now *Library Journal*, first mentioned expanding the librarian's duties to assist those seeking information, thereby increasing patron satisfaction and return visits to the library by providing resources and help.[2]

What actually happens at the reference desk is a mystery to many faculty and others. Few would consider what is done there to be "teaching" in the most basic meaning of the word. Why is that? One theory that I have discussed with many of my colleagues is how librarians are seen, and portray themselves, for lack of a better term, as skill-builders. A student stops by a reference desk to get quick, rather than comprehensive, help. Determining which database to choose, demonstrating how to find a review of a book, and helping with keyword searching and the like are low-level functions that don't belong on the continuum of learning. I'd like to see the word *skills* struck from our vocabulary. When we conduct the reference interview as an organic process, we have a distinct opportunity to guide students beyond skills-based efforts and encourage them toward a spirit of inquiry, learning, and self-sufficiency in the library setting. In my own library, my colleagues and I have worked assiduously to find a different way to talk about our reference work because we realized that the way we were perceived was counterproductive to our mission on campus. If there are misunderstandings and perception problems associated with what we do, it is the students who suffer. A faculty member who has little or no understanding of what goes on at the reference desk will be much less likely to send a student there. Faculty members who do not talk about the potential help that a reference librarian can offer not only deprive students of excellent research help, but also from developing a very important and integral campus alliance. Although students may encounter us in the classes we teach or the information literacy sessions that we do for faculty, the experience of sitting down with a librarian is invaluable because many students will not voice their frustration with the research process in front of a class.

The literature written about the need for reference pedagogy is rather delicious and thought-provoking. Not only does it make sense and encourage good practice, but it is also an important aspect to discuss when we come before promotion and tenure committees. Elmborg laments that "there has been very little discussion within the profession . . . about how to be an effective teacher at the reference desk, about how one teaches *well* as a reference librarian." He goes on to suggest that "academic librarians begin to see reference through the lens of educational psychology," citing the work of Doyle-Wilch and Miller, who advocate using "schemata theory" when teaching at the reference desk. This recommendation is based on "intellectual schemata" that are already at play when a student approaches the reference desk. They assert that "as humans move from experience to experience, they organize what they have learned from these situations and build upon personal knowledge." To me, this just seems to make good sense. Elmborg presupposes, too, that in the great tradition of Paulo Freire, we cede a bit of our own authority. We are those that sit across a desk, dispensing valuable knowledge and the deep, dark secrets of research strategies. We meet students where they are, and build on knowledge that they already possess but are unlikely to exhibit in the face of the "authority." Not a single student who comes to us is a *tabula rasa*—we have the unique opportunity to work *beside* the student to provide assistance.[3]

While we are teaching students at the reference desk, they are not beholden to us in any way: we are not grading them, criticizing their methods, or adding to their workload by assigning homework or papers. When we conduct the reference interview, we are eliciting information from students, providing them opportunities to voice their issues, problems, and the points at which they are stuck, rather than pontificating from the mountaintop. The point of articulation for students is invaluable. We may indeed be their first point of reference, because they lack the confidence to go to a professor for fear of disclosing inadequacies. It is important to know about the barriers to student learning, developing confidence, and working through problems, and attempt to not only address those issues at the reference desk, but also to use them as teaching moments on which to build a foundation.

At my university, we have many first-generation students. Although we understand the importance of reaching every student, it is essential to make connections with these first-generation students. Many have expressed total confusion about how the academic library works, and some (though not all) may come from families in which there was no culture of reading, library use, or even homework help. Some of these students come from charter schools or public schools that may not even have libraries, let alone databases from which to learn the fundamentals of research. When we can engage these students at the reference desk, we lay the foundation for learning as we build the network of people to whom they can go when classes become overwhelming as assignments involving research begin piling up.

Because librarians are no different than anyone else in that we tend to see most situations at the level of our own perception, it helps to look at reference through an educational lens rather than only through a service lens. I learned this lesson long ago, when for days I'd been tracking a student who seemed to be lost, endlessly, in the stacks. The first time I approached him, he quickly pulled a book off the shelf and opened it. "Finding everything okay?" I asked him. "Yeah," he mumbled. This took place in the chemistry section of the library, and I profiled him as an intense science major who didn't need my help. Another day, while unlocking study rooms on the second floor of our library, I saw him again, this time in the Pennsylvania history section. I watched his eyes roam the stacks from floor to ceiling. When I approached him to ask, this time more explicitly, if I could help him, he said, with a flip of the hair in his eyes, "How does this library work?" Just a few days before, because of my own ignorance I'd assumed that he'd found what he wanted. As I later learned when I invited him into my office to talk, he was not in fact a science major, but instead a first-year student who was an English major. I was curious whether his high school, which I'd never heard of, had a library. He told me that it did, but it used the Dewey Decimal system, which he thought all libraries did.

During the first meeting I initiated, I was able to explain the basics of how the library worked. In truth, I probably did little more than lay a foundation, but he learned who I was, that I was his liaison librarian, and that he'd be seeing a lot more of me. But at that first meeting, I gave him something to use immediately: an explanation of and a handout on the Library of Congress Classification system. I did not just model a teacher's behavior, but truly was a teacher in that moment. He was a rather humble and reserved student, and when he graduated I gently kidded him about how much he knew about the library in comparison to his first few weeks on campus. He laughed. I got a mention in his thesis (long before I was embedded in the English Thesis class) for my "invaluable help and kindness" during the research process.

I describe this event not in a self-congratulatory way, but instead to highlight how teaching happens in moments when we least expect it. It is not always a deliberate process, though we cannot deny our joy when encountering students who come to us on their own initiative, not because of a class requirement, and want to learn and are active during our meetings. I have been met with much reluctance from students while doing reference work, but I also know that professors who teach in the classroom face the same attitude day in and day out. I do not think this occurs because we are librarians, but rather I see it as students encountering "threshold concepts" that may cause them to feign indifference or sometimes even anger. It impedes learning if we take this personally. It is a scary proposition to encounter the unknown and must work to understand and empathize. A wonderful and unique aspect of academic librarianship is that students can come to us for help, knowing our personal agendas won't be in the way.

WAYS TO THINK ABOUT REFERENCE

Although I have been using the term *reference*, I am well aware that the basic reference model has changed in many academic libraries, and mine is no exception. The days when a librarian sat at a desk waiting for a student to stop by are long gone, replaced with a more active model of one-on-one research appointments and various other incarnations of service.

Finding a librarian at a desk can be incidental or deliberate, but tends to be more incidental. In my university library, we made the decision to get rid of the desk (well, not really—it now serves as a color print station) because we felt it was too passive for the librarians and too intimidating for the students. We've never looked back. We have found, collectively, that the quality of our reference or research sessions become stronger and more substantive and we were seeing more students than ever while still giving the same kind of help we always hoped to provide from behind that big circular desk!

Though there may be some who disagree, I feel that reference is reference, no matter where it is delivered. Engagement with students is the first, most fundamental, and foundational aspect that informs what comes next. If we do not engage with students, there will be no reference or teaching. During a reference transaction, we should approach them with the same attentiveness and mindfulness that we apply to our teaching.

The orientation of reference service in the United States has traditionally been what I will call "transactional," involving different interactions that may not be linear and indeed may be interrupted by the patrons themselves for a variety of reasons. Ranganathan, the father of library science, conceived of the practice as a holistic one that is the "primary motive and the culmination of all library practices."[4]

Ranganathan defined reference service as

> the process of establishing contact between a reader and his documents in a personal way. "His documents" means every one of the precise documents needed by him at the moment. It also means all the documents likely to be of use to him at the moment. It further means establishing the contact without any loss of time for him. It is not possible to do all this for a reader without an intimate understanding of his precise interest at the moment. To

get this understanding, there must be an intimate com-
munion between the librarian and the reader. From the
first moment of the reader asking for help to the last
moment of his getting all of his documents, the librarian
will have to be personally administering to the needs of
the reader. Therefore, reference service is essentially personal service.[5]

Marcia H. Chappell has argued compellingly that Ranganathan's theory "leaves no room for instruction as a function of reference service
in any kind of library." I disagree. Although Ranganathan's description of reference service is perhaps more ardent than we are comfortable with today, I can see instruction happening easily and organically
in Ranganathan's scenario. While he does not identify it as such,
delivering such "documents" (materials, information) to the reader
or researcher in a "personal way" describes, at least to me, an opportunity ripe for instruction to take place—even in its most basic form.[6]

FINAL THOUGHTS

Reference work is fundamental to librarianship. The academic library
setting is not only an essential component of assisting students to
learn how to find information, but also to evaluate and think critically about what they find.

Make no mistake, when a student approaches a reference librarian, a transaction will indeed take place, and more likely than not the
student will come away with something more than what he or she
began with.

Strategies

- Reference can be delivered in a variety of ways. Although
  in some places a traditional reference desk may be the best
  way to serve student needs, in others a more dynamic service
  model such as a combined service desk, a reference librarian

in a satellite location, or consultations by appointment may better serve the student population. Reference, like other library services, is changing and evolving. Explore to find out what is possible.

- Thinking of reference work as teaching will help to provide essential services. I will often ask students to take out a notebook and pen or to take notes on their phones. I use the reference transaction to *instruct*. Although this should seem obvious, I have spoken to a fair number of academic librarians who often encounter students who only want us to find whatever they are looking for. The idea is to teach students strategies that will help them over and over again.

- Email or instant messaging reference transactions can be challenging because we must conduct the reference interview in messages that require replies, a process with which students often lose patience. If, for instance, I ask a student "what have you tried already?" via email, the student is unlikely to respond because he or she wants immediate answers. I try to give students something—just enough so that they can see that there is more where that came from! It is a hook. Often I will arrange a time where I can meet with a student one-on-one. If not, I am sure to close the circle: in a day or two I will email the student to see how he or she made out with the information he or she found and if I can be of any further help.

- Consider keeping detailed notes on each reference transaction. I keep a log in which I enter the actual question and the steps I went through to help the student. I also make a note on my follow-up and its results. This has helped me to develop a praxis for myself and to make me aware of gaps in my current practice.

NOTES

1. James K. Elmborg, "Teaching at the Desk: Toward A Reference Pedagogy," *portal: Libraries and the Academy* 2, no. 3 (2002): 455–64.

2. Richard E. Bopp and Linda C. Smith, eds., *Reference and Information Services: An Introduction* (Santa Barbara, CA: Libraries Unlimited, 2011).

3. Elmborg, "Teaching at the Desk," 456.

4. Shiyali Ramamrita Ranganathan, *The Five Laws of Library Science*, (Madras, India: Madras Library Association, 1931).

5. Ravindra N. Sharma, *Ranganathan's Philosophy and Approach to Reference Service.* na 1988.

6. Marcia H. Chappell, "The Place of Reference Service in Ranganathan's Theory of Librarianship," *The Library Quarterly* 46, no. 4 (1976): 378–96.

3

Teaching and Learning
as Conversation

Knowledge creation is conversation.

—R. DAVID LANKES

As I sit here writing this chapter, I realize that when I think about my role as an academic librarian, I believe that conversation in both teaching and learning is preeminent. There are many facets of being a librarian, and I engage, as most of us do, in any number of them. However, as an academic librarian my thoughts focus on how I can initiate, facilitate, and deepen conversation in the classroom (or for that matter, anywhere I engage students) so that learning can happen. I have written and reflected a good amount on the topic and have engaged faculty and my librarian colleagues in "conversations about conversation" in order to emphasize how it promotes breakthroughs in student thinking, as well as modeling its value for myself and others.

GENESIS

I have an abiding belief that learning begins with conversation. Both my instinct and experience in the classroom tell me that when you engage students in conversation about their topics, you are often helping them in a way that gives voice to ideas that have just been rolling around in their heads, questions that they may be struggling with and not even know how to approach. When students engage with each other, they become part of what I have previously called a "community of scholars," that is, they join together to find meaning and contribute to knowledge—which is also how learning happens.

My fellow librarians and I have, over the years, spent untold amounts of time in meetings discussing information literacy, describing our personal approaches and practices and all that they encompass, but we particularly focus on how these impact our actual classroom teaching. There has been an evolution of practice, to be sure, as we have consistently reflected on our collective and individual practices over time. We have grappled with standardization; best practices; framework; one-shot instruction; and the discouraging lack of interest in our efforts from students and their professors, a situation that still stubbornly persists despite all of our strides in practice.

Years ago, everything in librarianship seemed to be in flux while simultaneously being evaluated and given dire prognoses. There were arguments about the role of librarians in the classroom and endless (though necessary) discussions of the best ways to deliver and assess information literacy. During that time, I began to seriously reevaluate my own practices as a librarian in the classroom. The times are still changing and the arguments are still continuing, and although I don't normally mind getting caught up in controversy, I have come to the conclusion that these endless debates divert attention from our current practice and our own agency. Instead, we need to think about how we can make a difference in our sessions, one class at a time. It doesn't require a mandate to reflect on our own practice and then try something different. Trust our own instincts? Absolutely. But trusting our instincts once was, and in some places still is, a radical act in the pedagogical practice in which librarians have been engaged.

When I was a new librarian teaching what were then called "bibliographic sessions," it was expected that the professor who asked you to come to class would both set and drive the agenda. In the beginning of my career, I found that comforting, because I was unsure of what I was doing and would not have known how to drive the agenda even if I had been asked. The professor always had clear expectations and prescriptions about what I was expected to deliver. Usually I was told to "show them databases, keyword searches, how to find a book." This was easy—too easy, in fact. I quickly became disillusioned playing the role of some sort of ersatz instructor who was merely auxiliary to the learning process. Often I was asked to come in too early in the semester (especially for freshman classes) and frontload everything that the professor thought would help his or her students. There were also times, when first meeting with students, I was expected to deliver my information literacy content *before* an assignment was even given! The students had no interest in instruction, especially when it was not tied to an assignment, because they did not perceive the need for any investment on their part. The professors' unconvincing exhortation to students to seek a librarian's help if they had difficulties had no focus. They seemed to wonder, "What do you even ask a librarian?" because they had little or no knowledge of how I actually *could* help them.

The ACRL Framework for Information Literacy for Higher Education is a recently revised information standard which illustrates that librarians are no longer (if we ever were) "point and click" instructors, but rather partners in the educational process both in and out of the classroom. The very basis of what we do in the classroom can be found in the conceptualization of ideas and the preparation to work with other realms of information and knowledge, all in the spirit of inquiry. I prefer this term to "research," because it implies an active and willing participation in knowing and understanding rather than merely amassing sources (in the form of downloaded articles). Not surprisingly, one of the frames in the framework is "research as inquiry."

I became increasingly frustrated because professors seemed happy to get library instruction out of the way as though it was an obligation, just something to check off the list, instead of a strategic and much-need information literacy collaboration. This went against my instinct, which was to walk into a class, work hard to make connections, and get a conversation going. *It was really as simple as that.* Interestingly, though perhaps not surprisingly, I came to understand that I could not just talk about collaboration with a professor who asked me to do a session in class. It didn't work like that. I created lesson plans that were unique and veered off the beaten path that professors expected. I covered what was needed—just not in the same way. My own credibility and that of my colleagues grew when we stopped merely talking about strategies and went ahead and enacted them in the classroom, showed concern for the needs of students, and strove to eliminate the type of one-shot instruction sessions that resulted when a professor asked a librarian to come to class and review numerous points or skills, including databases, keyword searching, and annotated bibliographies. It was impossible to cover everything, and I could sense that students got little out of these sessions beyond frustration. All instructors, including librarians, need time to build the trust, rapport, and relationships that make students receptive to learning. There was always pressure to cover too much in a single session. As a result, I began abbreviating my lessons and then asking the professor for another session, which, to my surprise, I was often given (albeit reluctantly). After a time, my strategy paid off and collaborations began to form, almost all of which continue to give me a tremendous sense of satisfaction.

PRACTICE

Because I have often been met with that glazed-over look from students, I decided to take a hands-off approach during my first (and often, subsequent) sessions in any given class. What that means, specifically—and this is important—is that the students and all of their attendant informational needs are, in that moment, more important than the technological tools and databases that both they and the professor expect me to explain. For this very reason, I prefer to hold my first session (of what will usually be a series of three) in a regular classroom instead of in a computer lab, where I will have to compete with large screens for attention. That means I get to look students in the eye, and they, too, get to size me up—and they do, to be sure.

They cannot hide behind a computer screen and I cannot use my bag of tricks: keywords, Boolean searches, and so on.

I have learned much about teaching from the great radical educator Paulo Freire, who rejected the "banking" system of education—the notion that we, the educators, stand up in front of a room and "deposit" knowledge into the heads of students who come to us as blank slates, with nothing to offer and everything to gain—that is, what we as the all-knowing librarian can give them. *I seek to do exactly the opposite.* I want to break down barriers and engage students in what *they* may be thinking. I will often begin with a conversation about their expectations for the session—which are usually pretty low—and I joke about how tired they look, how much coffee I just slugged down, that I know how difficult it is to go from an idea to a topic to a paper. *I empathize.* I give them permission to dwell in a phase of confusion and unknowing. I meet them where they are. They begin to open up. But more important than getting them to speak to me in class is getting them to speak with each other. *I encourage a loud class.* I like to pair them up and hear their conversations. I encourage crosstalk. I like to tag-team with students as they throw out ideas—I will add something and encourage others to do the same. We conceptualize out loud. We crowdsource for ideas, in order to mine the wisdom of the group. In this way the students can see for themselves how knowledge is made, which is not in the dark and dank vacuums of our own heads, where ideas not yet fully formed bump and bristle against one another. Knowledge happens *with* and *among* others. I never remind them to keep on topic—conversations go where they need to go. And often their conversations will take some arterial routes and go off the beaten path. In that case, I let them go where they think they need to go. For a time, students are "unplugged," which is a rare and a beautiful thing to behold.[1]

Not surprisingly, this approach has required me to teach with the courage of my convictions. If I am asked to a class because of my professional expertise, then I can act in partnership with the professor to come to an agreement on expectations, but I no longer take orders. Information literacy is not about service; it is about *learning*. Professors will often ask me, "What about databases? Keywords? Boolean searches?" I make it clear that all this cannot and should not be frontloaded into the first session and that students do not learn how to do research using searching strategies. Research is not a "search and find" problem—it is a problem of conceptualization and thinking. The constructivist approach works as we build on knowledge, first by tossing out ideas, then putting flesh on bare bones and providing a context for where to begin. We might say that the conversation that leads to conceptualization primes the pump. I encourage students to write down the ideas that come to them while we are all processing out loud—sometimes with a word or two and sometimes with sentences that they will access later. I tell them that ideas get tested in paragraphs, and that writing in narrative form will naturally encourage and generate more connections, more ideas.

Educational theories are continuously changing to reflect the times and places in which we and our students find ourselves. *This is a good thing.* Encouraging our students to begin to converse within themselves, with us, and with each other is far from radical, although it can seem so in the present climate of tools-based learning, where content knowledge is packed into databases just waiting to be unlocked with an imaginary magical key.

All learning begins with inquiry; of this there can be no doubt. J. F. Lyotard, the French philosopher, sociologist, and literary theorist, asks the questions all educators should ask themselves: "Can learning be transmitted? Facilitated? Through which medium?" When thinking about their approaches to information literacy, librarians may want to begin with what seems most natural for them. For me it was rejecting the popular "tools" approach (which is considered low-level) and, instead, working hard to get in touch with my students through conversation and by surveying the landscape of their thoughts. I encourage students to recognize that *progress is made through process.* One can, for instance, begin by creating a climate that is hospitable and safe for them to verbalize their thoughts, fears, and intellectual anxieties. What do students, at that moment in time, really need? We need to be mindful of the anxiety that students often feel around librarians, which in my opinion not only grows out of stereotypes, but also because they are not (and may have never been) very clear on what our role is. We can help by contributing to the conversation about explaining who we are and what they can

reasonably expect from us, both in and out of the classroom. Then
the conversation becomes reciprocal. If we ask them for honesty and
courage in putting forth their unformed ideas and thoughts, we must
do the same.[2]

According to Klipfel:

> This approach to understanding students' needs—where
> an information and educational need is taken to be equiv-
> alent to understanding a student's individual interests—
> suggests a shift in perspective on the part of the educator
> from viewing oneself as an expert transmitting informa-
> tion to others, to a student-centered focus where the edu-
> cator inhabits a more facilitative role.[3]

Kenneth Bruffee has written extensively about the importance
of conversation in education and learning. As he has astutely stated,
"Conversation is of such vital importance to learning that without it,
few of us would stand a chance." Conversation forges community,
and it is in community learning and support that individual learning
happens. This is the fuel behind what Klipfel terms *authenticity* in
learning and teaching.[4]

Karl Attard, who has written extensively on the reflection process, states that "conversing with someone else offers the possibility
of feedback and exposure to different viewpoints." Another lovely
byproduct is that by engaging students in conversation, librarians
lay the groundwork for students to make connections that will go
beyond a particular classroom experience. It almost always follows
that if a student can connect with you in class, he or she will be more
likely to seek out you or a colleague in the library after having begun
a conversation outside of it.[5]

When students can make connections with others in class, with
you as the facilitator of those conversations, they can begin to see
themselves think in the classroom and to build the muscle that critical thinking requires. Bechtel emphasizes the crucial role of librarians in both initiating and maintaining the conversation that nurtures
critical thinking:

> Appropriate response to the call of the university requires
> librarians who are educators—library educators, to be

sure, whose special and primary task is to facilitate scholarly conversation in the educational environment. Such
a role requires librarians who are or can become library
and educational generalists, whose critical facilities can be
continually honed and sharpened in the dialogue with faculty and students, who are themselves active in the life of
the mind and, above all who relish analysis and examination of significant issues.[6]

What Bechtel expresses is important, because we are just beginning
to see the value of conversation and, just as with other practices,
conversation works best when the librarian is fully committed to its
potential, not merely as an empty exercise (talk, talk, talk, and more
talk) but one that has immense pedagogical value and enhances the
learning experiences of students.

FINAL THOUGHTS

There are limits to what we can achieve in one, two, or even five
sessions of any given class, but there is much we can do. One is to
lay a foundation for students to create their own process, to show
them a way to begin, and to reassure them that it is okay that they
don't know what they don't know. Further, we can steer them in the
right direction so that they can say what they think, and hear what
they say, while receiving feedback that may take the form of questioning. This helps them to solidify their positions or rethink them
altogether. The hands-off approach respects student thought and
disabuses them of the idea that all they need to know can be found
by putting their hands on a computer keyboard—when actually it
begins within themselves.

In an age of technical rationality, we tend to favor what can be
proven, and that knowledge is in the domain of experts. When we
must rationalize the use of the tools we pay for, we should remember that, in the words of Parker Palmer, "When we think things
together, we reclaim the life force in the world, in our students and
in ourselves." Palmer goes on to state that the dangers of separating
teaching from learning is that it results in "teachers who talk but
do not listen and students who listen but do not talk." A holistic

classroom, ideally, will begin with conversation and end, quite possibly, in enlightenment and delight, for librarians, professors, and students alike. We have to be willing to suppress the strong—at times very strong—urge to be authoritarian, to jump in too soon with suggestions, or worse, to commandeer the conversation so that we can lead it where we think it should go rather than letting it find its own direction organically.[7]

Strategies

- It is okay for students not to know where to begin. I am convinced that the much-discussed and researched "library anxiety" is caused in part by the stereotype of the all-knowing librarian, against whom one's own knowledge might pale in comparison. Of course, *we* know that this isn't true, but students need to be reassured. When I repeat (perhaps too frequently) that students can come to see me even if they have no idea about the direction of their research, they are at first astonished because this is so different from what they usually are told: "to stand and deliver." I am true to my word. When I encounter students who have no idea where they are going, I do not see this as a deficit, but as an amazing place to begin. *Convince them this is true.* That confidence boost is propulsive.

- Suggest that students keep pen and paper handy. Although it might seem counterproductive to insist they take notes, gently prodding them during a breakthrough moment with "you might want to write that down" will be helpful when they later reflect on the conversation and remember that they uncovered a small gem.

- Give them something. But don't make it too easy! There is a balance between holding a conversation designed to prompt their own ideas and hanging them out to dry. Although we should not rush to fill the inevitable moments of silence, we can throw out points that they can latch onto, which might give them a pathway to further consideration, or to recognize an opportunity to deviate from or challenge a point they had previously sunk their teeth into. This shows give-and-take, which is, ultimately, what satisfying conversations are all about!

• Close the circle. I will wrap up a conversation by going over some points that we discussed and those that might have some traction. Either students will feel like they can get to the next level, or they won't. In either case, scheduling another conversation while they are right in front of you is a good idea: it shows a willingness to continue the conversation, conveys the worthiness of the discussion, and motivates students to do more thinking or digging before the next time you meet.

• There is always a way. If a student decides for one reason or another that he or she doesn't want to schedule another meeting, I wait a day and send an email reiterating my willingness to be of further help.

• Leave time for things to filter down. Students often feel as though they are expected to be totally self-sufficient—a byproduct of our individualistic national mentality, where the word *grit* is often bandied about, often to the shame of those who need or desire help. We are always responding at the level of our own perceptions. We are seasoned, while students are not—yet. They will come to understandings about their topics and their research, but that does not always happen in the timeframe we think is normal. Give them time to figure it out.

• Keep your own notes on the session. These are valuable not only for later reflection, but also to maintain continuity with the student. I not only keep notes on the content of a conversation, but also on the student's tone and demeanor, which usually tells me a great deal about where they are. Students are often heartened when they come back to see me and discover I can reference our meetings. It keeps that vital connection alive.

NOTES

1. Paulo Freire, *Pedagogy of Hope: Reliving Pedagogy of the Oppressed* (London; New York: Bloomsbury Publishing, 2014).
2. Jean-François Lyotard, Keith Crome, and James Williams. *The Lyotard Reader and Guide* (New York: Columbia University Press, 2006).
3. Kevin Michael Klipfel, "Authenticity and Learning: Implications for Reference Librarianship and Information Literacy Instruction," *College & Research Libraries* 76, no. 1 (2015): 19–30.
4. Kenneth A. Bruffee, "Collaborative Learning and the 'Conversation of Mankind,'" *College English* 46, no. 7 (1984): 635–52; Klipfel, "Authenticity and Learning."
5. Karl Attard, "The Role Of Narrative Writing In Improving Professional Practice," *Educational Action Research* 20, no. 1 (2012): 161–75.
6. Joan M. Bechtel, "Conversation, a New Paradigm for Librarianship?" *College & Research Libraries* 47, no. 3 (1986): 219–24.
7. Parker J. Palmer, *The Courage to Teach: Exploring the Inner Landscape of a Teacher's Life* (New York: John Wiley & Sons), 2017.

4

Promoting the Spirit of Inquiry in the Classroom

To think through or rethink anything, one must
ask questions to stimulate our thoughts.

—RICHARD W. PAUL AND LINDA ELDER

I have long been dissatisfied with the method of instruction expected from academic librarians. When we go into classrooms to instruct students in information literacy, we often know little more than the assignment at hand. We seldom know the students in front of us, or if we do, we know nothing of their work habits, their capabilities, their levels of interest in what they are being asked to do, or their feelings about virtually anything. This not only puts the librarian at a disadvantage, but can be potentially detrimental to students as well: we appear to want their attention and participation, but the circumstances in which we often meet them create difficulty and resistance. Our appearance in any given class or series of classes is highly dependent upon whether or not faculty members even want us there to begin with. And when they do, it often may be out of a sense that it is the right thing.

Sometimes I feel like little more than a working representative of proprietary databases: *click here, download there, print out.* Often this is because of what the faculty member requests—"Show them databases." Not surprisingly, when students are assigned a topic for research, their first impulse, perhaps out of anxiety, is to print out a veritable avalanche of research materials, which they then must sort through and, well, read! Inevitably, many will find that they cannot, for one reason or another, use what they've printed. As their anxiety escalates, it becomes more and more difficult for them to see a way out of their predicaments. Many students come to see librarians at just this point, when they have hit what they perceive to be a dead end. I have heard more times than I can possibly count that "there is nothing on my topic!" If no one else will say it, I will: searching for information is not that difficult. In the age of Google and databases, with so many different options ranging from full-text to peer-reviewed, searching is easy to *execute*. Then, you might ask, if searching is so easy, why do so many students end up with unusable or unacceptable results?

I have long thought that the problem comes from a student's unwillingness or inability to think through or carefully consider a topic, which translates to pounding the keyboard "to see what's out there." Students may feel personally disconnected from the assignment, especially those in which they have no personal interest. They often cannot connect their efforts to the idea that they are contributing to knowledge—they simply do not perceive research that way. But most of all, I see the difficulty as a lack of curiosity. Curiosity is naturally propulsive: when you are curious you are motivated to seek answers, which involves persistent questioning that will not only take you further in your understanding but often will send your research in another direction. Students may be frightened by this fluidity of process and are often unwilling to change course, especially if they have already printed out several articles and might feel as though that effort is wasted.

FOCUS ON INQUIRY

It is a daunting task to stand in front of a class of students and run through a repertoire of strategies in a 45-minute or hour-long class.

And if students have no context for the instruction that we are giving them (a particular assignment), they have nothing to anchor themselves and may not retain the instruction. I am an advocate for doing less in instructional sessions and instead focusing on high-yield strategies that build a foundation for the kind of research that students will need to do now and in the future.

What I have witnessed in my own classrooms and what other librarians and colleagues have shared with me is that students do not find research difficult only because of some supposed skills gap, for instance, that they do not know how to properly conduct database searches or use other sources to find information (although it may play a part). Rather, the root of the difficulty comes as a problem of *conceptualization*. I don't think that I can place too fine a point on this. The student, in an effort to replace the process of thinking, questioning, and conceptualizing, skips the important process of inquiry and relies entirely on concrete activities such as searching databases. This results in many undergraduates conducting the kind of research that they did for papers they wrote in high school: lots of facts reworded or regurgitated on the page. They ask few questions about their topics and issues, often because they feel as though they have nothing valuable to add to the conversation. Bruner asserted that learning, when it occurs, goes beyond the information given and creates what he called "products of the mind." The question then becomes: how do we get students to think beyond the information they are given?[1]

Donham, Kuhlthau, Oberg, and Bishop have written extensively about the process of inquiry in learning. They acknowledge the challenges of inspiring inquiry in students, stating that "students learn by constructing their own understandings of these experiences and by building on what they already know to form a personal perspective of the world." When we teach sessions, are we helping students to build on what they already know, or do we present prepackaged, predigested agendas that the students will either "get" or not?[2]

HOW THE RESEARCH PROCESS BEGINS

I am about to state the obvious: research begins with thinking. I can hear the groans already! Yes, intellectually we seem to understand this, but we do not necessarily put this into practice in the classroom.

To do so requires an approach very different than the one that we have been employing. It means encouraging questions before the research begins. What that looks like exactly is difficult to say—scenarios will differ. Alan Colburn has written about the particular behaviors that "promote inquiry-based learning":[3]

- Ask open-ended or divergent questions (such as "What are you doing?" "Tell me about what you are thinking," and "What do you think would happen if . . . ?").
- Wait a few seconds after asking questions in order to give the student time to think.
- Respond to students by repeating and paraphrasing what they have said without praising or criticizing. This encourages students to think for themselves, and to stop looking to the teacher for validation.
- Avoid telling students what to do, and avoid praising, evaluating, rejecting, or discouraging students' ideas and behaviors.
- Maintain a disciplined classroom.

When we are presented with a topic by the professor or students, we can begin to ask questions. I particularly love the question "tell me about what you are thinking," because it shows an ethic of care and creates a moment when we stop bombarding students with information and instead consider how they may be framing information. I have had more than a few breakthroughs with classes when I set my point-by-point agenda aside and listened while students expressed their understanding of a certain topic. They may have already formed ideas and made associations that can contribute to their understanding of the topic at hand. But what I have found interesting is that students have the misguided feeling that they should always know so much more than they do. This outlook will often keep them in a state of high anxiety and sends them running to databases before they have had the time to carefully consider their topics. They do not seek questions—they only want answers—the quicker, the better.

This lack of a sense of inquiry may be the root cause of students' focus on only looking for research that either proves or completely agrees with a thesis they have thought up without much consideration. This is due to a lack of confidence, yes, but also to a lack of curiosity, which I believe is stifled by fear. Curiosity, then, is a response to an information gap; it encourages critical thinking by closing gaps one by one, and, more often than not, opening up new ones that will then be closed in the same way. It is an iterative process that moves critical thinking forward, and can continue until the last paragraph of the paper is written. The librarian's presence in the classroom is often not considered valuable by students, who may have heard from others that the sessions are pointless and boring. In the words of one former reluctant library user, "Why bother paying attention? If I need help, I'll just go get it when I need it." The scenario is very different when the instruction encourages engagement and is participatory and respectful, one where *not knowing* is welcome and space is made for questions. As librarians, we can identify some of the gaps in class conversation with students, and then they will often themselves identify gaps in conversation with each other.[4]

HELPING TO GENERATE QUESTIONS

Not too long ago, I met with a small literature class of six students. The students had been working with three texts and were assigned to write a paper on any one of them. Although the professor had asked me to give the standard databases drill, after one minute in the class I knew that I had already lost them, and that it would be extremely difficult to do what he wanted. He chided them a bit, and then jokingly threatened to increase the paper's length by three pages. *Still nothing.* On a dismal winter day (and an 8:30 a.m. class on top of it!), I stood in front of these students and felt annoyed. They seemed so disengaged that it verged on rudeness. I began the class by tentatively asking questions. One student in the class mumbled something with a pen in her mouth, but I very much appreciated the effort. I repeated what she had said and then asked the class, "What do you think she meant by that? You could look at it in a few different ways." The responses came slowly. I was careful not to fill in the silences, because I wanted to leave the students space for their thoughts. I wanted to encourage questioning by allowing them to do just that: create questions. I had told them, and then gently reminded them at least one other time, that I was not interested in answers, but about thoughts that might turn into questions. The professor was himself a bit anxious, watching the clock and likely thinking that what I was doing was pointless. This was probably not because my method was bad—this is a typical way to encourage inquiry in the classroom—but more so because he felt that it was his job, not mine, to engage them in this way. I asked the students to get out their notebooks or a piece of paper and begin "chaining" their questions, encouraging them to probe further and deeper. Knowledge is not created in a vacuum and neither are questions, so I also asked them to talk to each other. While they did that, I pulled up the library homepage so that we could begin to navigate some databases. They worked on refining questions that reflected curiosity so that they weren't asking simple questions and then looking for simple answers. It does not take long for students to begin to give each other ideas (which seems to be easier with someone else's topic than their own), which almost always ends up helping them to see their own topics in a new light. Talking about their ideas and their roadblocks can be just what they need to get started. This is a different way of beginning the research process: respecting the questions themselves that will support and propel the research forward, instead of making a mad dash to find answers in downloaded articles with titles that seem to speak to their immediate needs. But it is not enough to leave students to question by themselves. We must encourage that questioning, as Kelley-Mudie and Phillips propose, by "making a space" for questions and questioning. Too often we respond to students in a way that acts "as if"—as if they should know how to begin, or as if they should already know how to generate keywords, because librarians view the process from our own high level of expertise. We can help to mediate questions, to ask questions that will help students to think more deeply in some cases and more broadly in others. We can help them to make distinctions and correlations that some may find difficult to do in the early stages.[5]

Librarians are in the unique position of being able to show students how questioning is their entrée into research. It seems so simple to us that we must first ask a question, but this is not evident to students. Each time we get in front of a classroom and go straight to databases, we presuppose that students have already worked out everything in their heads or that they will soon figure it out. This is one of the reasons why so many of us who encounter the same students again and again feel as though nothing we have taught them sticks. I have repeatedly sat across from students who I have seen in several sessions in other classes, and it feels as if we begin from scratch each time. I have often said, good-naturedly, something along the lines of "I remember I covered this in your EN202 class!" It isn't difficult to understand why this could be a source of burnout in librarians. I have often felt incredibly frustrated by this aspect of teaching information literacy sessions. I realized that if students cannot find something in the topic to connect with personally, it will be difficult for them to form the fundamental curiosity necessary to keep them going. Bruner believed that it is not enough for students to merely gather information (which has been made incredibly easy by the plethora of information available at the touch of a keystroke). True learning requires more—it entails going beyond compiled information. Students must understand that learning involves many different mental processes, far outside the reaches of the most obvious questions and answers. Teaching ourselves how to marinate in our ideas, to turn them around and view them from all sides, to slice them open like a cross-section, or to put a fire to them and see what they do—this is where student curiosity can thrive. It is an incredibly important and time-consuming part of the research process, but one on which librarians seldom linger because of the restrictions on the time and frequency we have to meet with any given class, not to mention what a professor may tell us to teach the students. This almost mirrors the difficulties students already have, because, according to Kuhlthau and colleagues, "the early stages [of research] are often hurried, and the middle stages often frequently passed over as students are urged to collect and complete their work." Because information literacy or bibliographic instruction is our realm of expertise, librarians can make a case that lingering in the inquiry phase with students is not only worthwhile in the short term, but can also yield long-term results because it creates a *habit of learning* that begins in inquiry and respects the process on the road to discovery. It is not just a search for cut-and-dried answers, but for understanding and knowing.[6]

VALUING AND MODELING PROCESS

When writing about the process of information seeking, Gloria J. Leckie plainly states what many research librarians have undoubtedly observed in many classrooms with many students: that students are continuously in a mode of "coping when they are conducting information searches, not, in fact, engaging in an information-seeking strategy." This constant mode of coping is the antithesis of a strategy and it behooves librarians to understand this about student behavior.[7]

Kuhlthau's Information Search Process model gives us insight into the stages of the research process within both the cognitive and affective aspects of student information searching. It is with the *thinking*, not the searching, that students have difficulty; it is the *conceptualization* that they struggle with, not how to use databases. The seven-step process is as follows:[8]

1. **Initiation** occurs when a research topic is introduced, and students must think up an engaging question or series of questions to begin the process. This initial stage is greatly enhanced by engagement and assistance in the classroom from the librarian and/or the librarian and professor. This stage lays the foundation for the search process.

2. **Selection** requires the all-important decision-making that is part of any search process. Here students will begin to parse out what they may (or may not) already know about their topics. They should be urged to examine what it is that they really want to discover.

3. **Exploration** occurs when students begin to venture out into more inquiry, developing more questions that will guide them to seek information. This is said to be the most difficult stage of the research process because it requires action, not just conceptualization. Students will feel anxious and doubtful about their ability to find the information that they need.

4. **Formulation** is the stage in which students begin to form their own perspectives on their topics, which will include "dimensions, issues, and ramifications" of their subject.

5. **Collection** is the stage where there is potential to build confidence during the research process as students apply their formulated questions to create searches to yield the information they've been seeking. They now begin to attain "a sense of ownership and expertise" with their subject.

6. **Presentation** is the culmination of all the preceding processes. In this stage, students will present their information in the form required (paper, presentation, etc.).

7. **Assessment** is the stage where students reflect on their process and what they have learned, and what they can improve in the future.

It is important to remember that in contrast to scholars or faculty members, when students search for information, they have only a short amount of time needed to relax into the process and required to fulfill each stage. As a result, students skip the inquiry stage, which is essential, and go right to the gathering stage where they feel trapped and under the gun to come up with something, indeed, anything at all. Kuhlthau emphasizes that librarians often only focus on the *identification* of resources without properly preparing students to think about what they might need based on their questions and then how to interpret that information. Students want and expect a linear progression, but there is nothing remotely linear about a search process. Personally, I like to state this to students right up front to disabuse them of any notion that everything will proceed in a straight line. I often illustrate my process by showing them a scribbled mess on a whiteboard or a piece of paper—which is very much what a search process actually looks like! This takes some time for students to understand, and modeling it for them helps.[9]

Still, although we can tell students that the process is not linear, many will be impatient not only with themselves, but also with the process. Bodi states that "generally, students want enough information to meet the needs of their assignment and they want it without delay, thereby selecting full text articles and ignoring mere citations. Their lack of patience may say more about their perspective on the value of research and their schedule and less on the impact of technology." Librarians can help to guide students through the process, which will admittedly be unique to each student. This will in turn reveal the process to be just that—a process—and assure them that they will acquire what they need if only they would dwell in what can be an uncomfortable place for a bit.[10]

Bodi recognizes that the limitations librarians face in the classroom, where we must work with students who are not "ours" and content that we have not created and will neither teach nor grade, has made librarians "question their appropriate role in instruction." These very challenges brought me to a new way of thinking about research, both in general and from the viewpoints of students at many different levels and in different classroom situations. I essentially overhauled my entire method of conducting information literacy sessions and how I carried out my one-on-one meetings with students. When we are in front of a classroom guiding a group of students through the research process students, we are, as MacAdam emphasized, learning to "think in a new way, to question, to challenge, to keep, to discard, and to analyze information."[11]

FINAL THOUGHTS

Librarians can foster a spirit of inquiry in the classes they teach by approaching each session or one-on-one with intentionality and respect for process. For years we have been treating information literacy as tool-based instruction and missing many essential steps. We have also been attempting to teach too much—too many skills, databases, and strategies—in our sessions, leaving many students with a very real sense of bewilderment and lack of confidence. The process of inquiry is foundational, and knowing how to ask the right kinds of questions at the outset strengthens the foundation for all subsequent learning thereafter and increases student confidence. Committing ourselves to this approach to instruction, ideally in collaboration with faculty, can in many ways revolutionize instruction in general.

Strategies

- Understand the research process from a student's point of view.
- Acknowledge and communicate to students that you understand the difficulties inherent in research.
- Encourage students to probe and interrogate their subjects, topics, and issues and to formulate questions based on what they genuinely want to know.
- Mediate and facilitate the generation of questions.
- Pair students up to discuss their topics with one another and to discover aspects of a topic that neither of them might have thought of individually.
- Encourage or require students to write down their thoughts and ideas using bullet points, concept maps, or narrative to capture lightbulb moments as they occur, which will also show the progress from one idea to the next.
- Engage in active conversations with faculty to discuss whether you can teach more than one session per class so that the encouragement of inquiry can be followed by more concrete strategies. Ask for a syllabus and assignment in advance. Challenge any requests to teach a session that is not directed at a specific assignment.

NOTES

1. Jerome S. Bruner, *Acts of Meaning*, vol. 3 (Cambridge, MA: Harvard University Press, 1990).
2. Jean Donham, Carol Collier Kuhlthau, Dianne Oberg, and Kay Bishop, *Inquiry-Based Learning: Lessons from Library Power* (Worthington, OH: Linwood, 2001).
3. Alan Colburn, "An Inquiry Primer," *Science Scope* 23, no. 6 (2000): 42–44.
4. Ian Leslie, *Curious: The Desire to Know and Why Your Future Depends on It* (New York: Basic Books, 2014).
5. Sara Kelley-Mudie and Jeanie Phillips, "To Build a Better Question," *Knowledge Quest* 44, no. 5 (2016), 14.

6. Jerome S. Bruner, *Beyond the Information Given: Studies in the Psychology of Knowing* (New York: W. W. Norton, 1973); Donham, Kuhlthau, Oberg, and Bishop, *Inquiry-Based Learning*.

7. Gloria J. Leckie, "Desperately Seeking Citations: Uncovering Faculty Assumptions about the Undergraduate Research Process," *The Journal of Academic Librarianship* 22, no. 3 (1996): 201–08.

8. Donham, Kuhlthau, Oberg, and Bishop, *Inquiry-Based Learning*.

9. Carol Collier Kuhlthau, "Developing a Model of the Library Search Process: Cognitive and Affective Aspects," RQ (1998), 232–42.

10. Sonia Bodi, "How Do We Bridge the Gap between What We Teach and What They Do? Some Thoughts on the Place of Questions in the Process of Research," *The Journal of Academic Librarianship* 28, no. 3 (2002): 109–14.

11. Bodi, "How Do We Bridge the Gap between What We Teach and What They Do?"; Barbara MacAdam, "Sustaining the Culture of the Book: The Role of Enrichment Reading and Critical Thinking in the Undergraduate Curriculum," *Library Trends* (Fall 1995).

5

Collaboration with Faculty

Coming together is a beginning; keeping together
is progress; working together is success.

—HENRY FORD

The professional uneasiness that continues to exist between librarians and the faculty with whom we teach is legendary and deeply entrenched. There are a myriad of reasons for this, and an untold number of articles written on this subject that frame it as a problem, but it can also be seen as an opportunity. Assuming that most librarians want to collaborate with faculty, it is incumbent on us to see this opportunity and work to achieve this goal. Librarians are indispensable to faculty, and ultimately share the same goal: helping students in any way possible to succeed. Early in my career, I could not shake the feeling of being "lesser than" faculty in whose classes I taught. I felt disrespected on a number of occasions, which not only made me angry but lessened my confidence in front of a class, particularly when I felt I was being used to fill up some time for an ill-prepared instructor, or to act as a placeholder for a faculty member attending a conference. I have often been asked to speak to a class because it was considered an item to be checked off the semester list and then immediately forgotten.

Perhaps we librarians have done ourselves a disservice by continually advertising ourselves as "service providers." I have often tried to reason with colleagues and others that anyone working with students in a university or college setting is, technically, a service provider. Faculty certainly provide services to students in the form of teaching, advising, grading, and myriad other activities. Yet the teaching aspect of librarianship has yet to be fully embraced or understood by faculty and others in university settings, but also by librarians themselves.

CONTEXT

Although there are many reasons for both the real and perceived lack of full collaboration between librarians and faculty, one major stumbling block is the traditional emphasis on the idea that librarians teach low-level "skills" in contrast to the high-level "knowledge" that is the main currency of faculty, which they clearly see as their domain.

Despite the fact that on my campus librarians have faculty status and are eligible for promotion (but not tenure), we are still seen as a sort of exception—the same, but different. At times, this has seemed like an uphill battle for acceptance and recognition. But if we are perceived as true colleagues rather than mere ancillaries to the faculty, we have greater potential for helping students to realize their educational goals. A shared vision is one of the most important features of collaboration, and from experience I can say that partnering and collaborating with faculty create a much more meaningful learning experience for students.

Initially, I had been trying to prove myself while at the same time trying to fulfill all the demands and expectations of certain faculty members. I became resentful and lacked confidence because I did not feel as though I could protest or say no. What I was doing in an attempt to be cooperative and collegial was reinforcing that I *was* ancillary to the process and that my profession was merely in service to the rest of the faculty. Meulemans and Carr describe the ways librarians often rationalize what they are willing do for faculty, even though it may clash with their professional or pedagogical instincts:[1]

- But at least I get in front of the students.
- I want the professor to know I can be helpful.
- It's the students who will suffer if I don't do it.
- Even if they only get a little out of it, it's worth it.
- Students will know that the library is a friendly place.

I, too, had fallen into the trap of rationalizing until I realized it was getting me nowhere, and only served to widen what faculty perceived as a gap between themselves and librarians. Agreeing to the faculty's demands for poorly thought-out classes is exactly opposite to the kind of collaboration that students benefit from and that we want to facilitate. Meulemans and Carr suggest we not only be emboldened to say no to what they call "ill-conceived requests," but that collaboration begins, or has greater potential when we go further than the "no" and "question, engage and converse" with faculty, which requires going beyond our comfort level. It is only when we stand firm in our own mandate and assert ourselves as the professionals we are that the roots of collaboration can begin to take hold.[2]

WHAT IS COLLABORATION?

Collaboration can be a rocky path. It is, however, essential for librarians everywhere to be open and receptive, even when those with whom we want or need to collaborate are resistant. Collaboration is an essential connection between two or more parties who share a common goal and work toward achieving that goal in the most cooperative way possible. It goes without saying that this is not always easy, but it is almost always worthwhile. Mattessich and Monsey offer a more formal definition of collaboration: "Collaboration is a mutually beneficial and well-designed relationship entered into by two or more [individuals or] organizations to achieve common goals." If we examine the components of this definition, which is as good as any that I have seen, we can say that our "common goal" is the education of the student; the "well-designed relationship" is one that is intentional and will be nurtured and maintained; and the "mutually beneficial" aspect is that both parties must be satisfied with the methods and outcomes of the collaboration. Faculty and librarians alike benefit greatly from collaboration—faculty need us to instruct their students, and we would not have jobs if we didn't! Of course, I am being a bit facetious and simplistic in my explanation, but if we boil it down, that is as foundational as it gets![3]

Further validation of the interdependence of mission is the assertion made by Raspa and Ward, who assert that "we have reached a point at which neither librarians nor instructional faculty can adequately teach the research process in isolation from each other." With that said, it is often incumbent upon librarians to take the lead in actively showing instructional faculty exactly what it is that we do. The days of waiting to be recognized for our expertise or being asked specifically for our advice in a given class are over. This requires we adopt a mindset that is very different from that of the traditional, passive librarian, in which we do what we are told to do, simply respond to requests for instruction, and provide little or no input. And yet, much to my bewilderment, many librarians still resist taking a more active stance in emphasizing our expertise! Why? Faculty may have heard of information literacy, but not all of them have worked with its precepts or understand it at the level of academic librarians. I became aware of this years ago when every session I was asked to give only involved demonstrating pertinent databases, which students often thought were out of sync with assignments or other projects. In those dreaded one-shot deals, I stood in front of classes with so many things to show them, fully aware that none would stick. Many faculty still do not understand how well-positioned librarians are to help integrate learning in the classroom and some may feel threatened by our mere presence. We may also be working with faculty who themselves have no idea how to use library resources because the majority of their research was done before the advent of the internet and the plethora of online information and databases currently available, or they are no longer engaging actively in any research (or they have graduate assistants who do it for them). Interestingly, in many sessions that I have taught, the professors ask most of the questions.[4]

COURSE DESIGN

Collaboration has the potential to occur on a number of levels. Years ago at my university, we felt that one of the best ways to implement our information literacy plan was to collaborate with instructors in the university's first-year seminar classes, which were a requirement for all first-year students. We felt, and thankfully the faculty agreed, that it would best serve students if we had frequent contact with first-year students in the classroom. This would lay the foundation for students to form relationships with faculty librarians that would carry over into other classes and other assignments. Each librarian was assigned a number of classes and instructors to work with. Although not every instructor was interested in deliberately scaffolding information-literacy strategies and instruction into the syllabus, those that did were (and still are!) wonderful to work with. Each year, our involvement grew more and more as various assessments proved the collaboration was fruitful for all involved. Instructors were able to see that students benefited from our instruction because it was strategic and thoughtful, in contrast to the on-the-fly or one-shot sessions that many had thought were sufficient—even though they proved, over and over, not to be!

Interestingly, some instructors were so receptive that they welcomed us to take a look at their syllabi and discuss where, how, and how often we thought it best to be involved in the class. Others felt the need to hold on to more control, some initially and others for an entire semester, and made suggestions of their own to see if we would agree. What my colleagues and I have learned over the years is that much of collaboration is based on relationships and goodwill—in my experience, everything else follows from that. I am of the opinion that good relationships make good collaborations, but there are those who don't see it that way. Badke calls the quest for a relationship with faculty the "librarian as friendship evangelist" and sees attempts at friendliness as "wheedling" our way into a faculty member's good graces, and believes that this approach comes from a point of weakness. We will sometimes win small victories, maybe even the occasional big one, but there are no guarantees that faculty will return the consideration. You could apply that theory to any relationship at all.

Librarians aren't looking for guarantees that a faculty member will have our backs, but rather for the friendly relationships and mutual respect needed to work together for the greater good of students. This sometimes requires diplomacy, but we must assert our expertise by offering suggestions and alternate views as needed. Although it was hard-won, our involvement in first-year seminars helped us to build solid relationships with teaching faculty. In time they began to see our expertise and capabilities with new eyes, which, not surprisingly, paved the way to other areas on campus previously thought of as the domain of traditional faculty. Meulemans and Carr assert that "if instruction librarians fail to engage faculty in a collaborative manner, no amount of marketing or superficial outreach will help to create the partnerships we so desire." Often this means that librarians may need to take the lead and initiate the first steps toward collaboration with faculty. In essence, we must teach them how to work with us and to involve us on different collaborative levels.[5]

SUBJECT LIAISON OPPORTUNITIES

Although what subject liaisons look like will vary in among academic libraries, they will find immense opportunities to collaborate with the faculty of their institutions. I am lucky in my present position to have seen the evolution of librarian and faculty collaborative relationships. At the beginning of my career ten years ago, there was very little, if any, collaboration. Librarians were not seen as equal at any level. What we did was a mystery to most, though a few professors were curious enough to find out more as long as they held on to their budgets for books and databases and were able to add to their collection. When I inherited the English department as my main liaison area, I wanted the department faculty to know who I was and how I could best help them and their students. But I was also very keen on collaborating with them. I showed interest by carefully cultivating professional relationships that I hoped would not only grow, but flourish. It took a lot of time and I struggled with feelings of inadequacy and often felt a bit servile. My effort seemed immense in relation to what I was getting in return. But reflecting on my actions helped me to see that it wasn't all about me, and it wasn't all about them, either. Ultimately, I was seeking a greater role in order to reach students in a different and fuller way. And I couldn't achieve that without collaborating with faculty.

I also took an interest in faculty research. I "interviewed" each full-time faculty member in my liaison department. I did this in a few ways, always conscious of keeping things friendly and casual. Sometimes I would invite them to my office, where I would offer coffee or tea. I might show up at their offices with a coffee and scone in hand; if they were busy, I told them to enjoy their day. Then I would follow up by email to see when would be a good time to stop by. Interestingly, my colleagues seemed to think that I lost out if I dropped off hot coffee and a pastry to a faculty member who didn't have time to meet with me. One former colleague told me, "if meeting with them is so important, I am surprised you were not more strategic." I understood where she was coming from, but my goal was to create goodwill. I almost always was able to go back after making an email connection. I wasn't bothered the few times I wasn't able to do so, because I considered my efforts to be, as the cliché goes, more of a marathon than a sprint.

The conversations that I eventually had with the department's faculty were many and varied. I was genuinely interested in them as people, as well as their scholarship: the books they were writing, the research they were doing, the grants they were pursuing, the proposals they were writing. I made careful notes on all of this, then began an information file on each faculty member, which helped me reach out when a book, a conference, an award, or other research opportunities came to my attention. Remember that at this time I was still being asked, sporadically at best, to come to random classes with little or no thought given to how or if my instruction would line up with student learning. This rankled, of course, and more than a few times I felt as though my efforts were getting me nowhere. However, I stayed the course.

I would like to say that eventually all saw the light and it was unicorns and meadows once they finally opened their eyes to see how wonderful I was and how integral my expertise was to their own missions. But it wasn't like that then and isn't now. Nor, really, did I need or want it to be.

I have read so much of the research that talks about the resistance that faculty have to librarians, and can see the results. However, what I see now is not so much resistance—for that, faculty would have to think of us much more than they do. In reality, we are often invisible until they need us. Now, my efforts were paying off. I was no longer invisible. I inserted myself in many places that made me feel uncomfortable, but that didn't stop me from doing so.

For instance, at the beginning of a semester I asked to attend the first English department meeting for ten minutes so I could address all of the faculty at once and everyone would hear what I had to say at the same time. My goal was to be able to talk about more than my traditional liaison role, which had primarily and historically focused on collection development for the department, but also to explain my desire to get into their classes to help students with research. I had to show how that would be different, fuller, deeper, and broader than what I was already doing. I had asked for ten minutes, which seemed more than reasonable. *They gave me five.* But, with face flushed, I made the most of those five minutes and then followed up with each professor by email. But instead of just sending a follow-up email that repeated what I had already said, I asked each of them to send me syllabi for any or all of the courses that they were teaching. This helped me to see more clearly what I could offer that would be most helpful. Not all, nor even most, but many faculty did share this information with me, which helped me to develop a list of questions specific to each syllabus that showed how the student could research particular assignments.

I was slowly gaining ground and I could feel it. This feeling was generative: it made me want to go further and expend more energy because I was finally getting a return on my investment! Admittedly, it was not as fast or as full as I thought it should be, nor as much as I thought it could be, but it was an improvement from where I began. Although to some my methods may seem a bit servile and demonstrated exactly what I admonished against at the beginning of this chapter, I considered (and still do) that what I was doing was outreach, plain and simple.

My reason for giving the preceding example of my own experience is to show the evolution of how collaboration can be achieved.

When I first began as the liaison librarian for the English department, my predecessor, a wonderful, intelligent, and hard-working librarian, was doing all that she then could, and as our roles on campus grew, she was carefully positioning herself to do more. When she left to take a leadership position at another university, I became the new face of this initiative. What the faculty really wanted was to continue what the previous liaison had been doing, which had been limited because they limited her. I was met with a lot of opposition, but small changes added up to big ones over time. In the meantime, my colleagues were struggling with their own departments as they tried to accomplish similar things. Initially outcomes varied, but we reasoned that success for one of us meant success for all of us.

THE OPPORTUNITY OF BEING EMBEDDED

Although I already have written an entire book on embedded librarianship, I could not keep the topic out of a chapter focusing on collaboration with faculty. Paradoxically, the last place that I thought would present an opportunity for collaboration, let alone a successful one, was as the embedded librarian in an English capstone course. The stuff dreams are made of—well, a professional librarian's dreams, anyway![6]

If necessity is the mother of invention, then my entrée into the embedded classroom was borne out of keenly observing English thesis students and discovering what they needed. I was genuinely dismayed that seniors in a major whose chief activity is writing of research papers still had extreme difficulty doing so. I reasoned that four years of library instruction during their tenure in college, haphazard as it may have been, should have taught them something about research. But again, because these sessions were often ill-conceived and ill-timed by faculty, students had not learned how to conduct research in any meaningful way.

I kept one-on-one thesis consultation notes and began to see a pattern of difficulties that all focused on the same things: conceptualization, keywords, narrowing down an idea, and identifying the experts on their chosen texts. Upon presenting this information to a faculty member who was very close to retirement (and who I thought was overly proprietary about the class), he assured me that, on the one hand, he thought his students knew what they were doing, but on the other, he lamented their lack of focus. I knew about these problems because I was seeing a majority of these students in one-on-one consultations. This type of consultation was a true sign that the students were having difficulties. In general, a majority of this kind of consultation came from requirements that students see a librarian—but his students were not required to do so.

When I spoke with the professor, I shared my notes with him and, not knowing much about embedded librarianship myself, merely followed my instinct that it would be great if I could be in the classroom with the students to hear what they were hearing and try to understand the level at which they were reacting to that information. The word *embedded* was not yet in my mind, but the phrase *being there* was. Shortly thereafter the two began to come together. In certain ways, embedded librarianship can be seen as the pinnacle of collaboration, and it can take a while to achieve. I became embedded in what I would call "gradations." Although I am now fully embedded, and involved in the class in every way each fall semester, I can now see that such a collaboration could have never existed, would have never even been thought possible, without all of what felt at the time to be the tedious steps required to build a foundation. After this shift in mindset, we can begin to see that everything then becomes an opportunity for collaboration. Meulemans and Carr state that

> Even though it is disciplinary faculty that initiate the context for library instruction, that does not diminish the necessity of librarians taking equal, and if necessary primary agency in the construction of the learning environment for students. Establishing this agency may require a response and a subsequent conversation that are far different from what the faculty may be expecting, but far closer to what quality collaborative teaching can be.[7]

Once you are positioned, collaboration will feel less artificial and fraught, and instead full of possibility. Being embedded in a capstone, research writing, or other foundational course can be an incredibly powerful experience for all involved.

FINAL THOUGHTS

Collaboration will remain one of the greatest challenges of academic librarianship. Thankfully, though getting to that place may prove to be challenging for many of us, it is certainly a much smoother road to travel than it was even just a few years ago. Now, with students as well as teaching faculty struggling to keep up with a rapidly changing information landscape, opportunities for collaboration across the board will improve.

What I have put forth here is not mean to be exhaustive, but instead to show instances in which some collaboration may be untried, but would be good to take a chance on. Although I fully realize that collection development is most definitely a collaborative affair between faculty and librarians, I have not included it in this discussion because it is the one collaboration that is traditional, and in which faculty most often interact with librarians. This collaboration is very important, and most librarians engage in it on one level or another. It is, for lack of a better term, "low-hanging fruit."

Our own personal attitudes toward our profession, our students, and the faculties with whom we seek to collaborate are all impacted by what Meulemans and Carr's term a "professional value system," the response to which will depend upon "who is on the receiving end of the inquiry." They further state that "when a librarian's professional value system is centered on being partners in the teaching/learning endeavor, her actions fundamentally change." Our actions *do* change as we work hard to join forces with teaching faculty, have the difficult conversations, and put in the work. After all, the goal is the same: the education of our students.[8]

Strategies

- Be an active member of campus. *Be seen.* But *see others,* too.
- Attend faculty meetings. Usually you will have time before and after the meeting to mingle in a relaxed and congenial setting. Coffee may be involved!

- Introduce yourself to new faculty members in your department and consider inviting them to lunch or giving them a personal tour of campus.

- Consider brown-bag lunches with faculty in the library (with a limit of five to seven faculty) who might want to talk about changes in the library, equipment, collections, and so on.

- When meeting with faculty members one-on-one, consider hosting them in your office or the library, where you are on familiar ground and can make them feel welcome.

- Don't be afraid to talk about yourself. Although you certainly do not want to come off as egotistical, or monopolize the conversation, getting to know someone involves learning about him or her by showing interest and sharing a bit of yourself, too. See if you can find common points of interest with the faculty member even if it is not something based in academia. One faculty member that I found rather intimidating also had a daughter in college who kept switching majors. Instantly relatable!

- If you speak of your faculty colleagues, speak well of them. Just as the one being gossiped about will eventually be told what others are saying, so will compliments and genuine regard. It is difficult to resist the efforts of someone who admires you.

- Be strategic. Know when an "ask" is simply asking too much. Although I firmly believe that we often must take the lead and believe in ourselves enough to make a case for collaboration, sometimes, for a myriad of reasons, it may not be the right time or the right class. The idea is collaboration, not an all-out attempt to establish our own agenda.

- Be open to all possibilities as they present themselves—because they *will* present themselves!

NOTES

1. Yvonne Nalani Meulemans and Allison Carr, "Not at Your Service: Building Genuine Faculty-Librarian Partnerships," *Reference Services Review* 41, no. 1 (2013): 80–90.
2. Ibid., 81.
3. Paul W. Mattessich and Barbara R. Monsey, *Collaboration: What Makes It Work. A Review of Research Literature on Factors Influencing Successful Collaboration* (Saint Paul, MN: Amherst H. Wilder Foundation, 1992).
4. Dick Raspa and Dane Ward, *The Collaborative Imperative: Librarians and Faculty Working Together in the Information Universe* (Chicago: Association of College and Research Libraries, 2000).
5. William B. Badke, "Can't Get No Respect: Helping Faculty to Understand the Educational Power of Information Literacy," *The Reference Librarian* 43, no. 89–90 (2005): 63–80; Meulemans and Carr, "Not At Your Service."
6. Michelle Reale, *Becoming an Embedded Librarian: Making Connections in the Classroom* (Chicago: American Library Association, 2015).
7. Meulemans and Carr, "Not at Your Sevice," 88.
8. Ibid.

6

Critical Librarians and Critical Pedagogy in the Classroom

For apart from inquiry, apart from the praxis, individuals cannot be truly human. Knowledge emerges only through invention and re-invention, through the restless, impatient, continuing, hopeful inquiry human beings pursue in the world, with the world, and with each other.

—PAULO FREIRE

Critical pedagogy in the classroom is now more important than ever. Even a cursory glance at the news headlines each day reveals the need to empower students in deliberate and conscious ways as a bulwark against the many and various forms of oppression, be they blatant and some insidious.

As a librarian, I have often envied professors who, in their own classes, are able to apply any number of critical pedagogical strategies to any number of subjects. It took me some time to see how I could do the same in my bibliographic instruction classes and other encounters with students. This is called *critical librarianship*. It employs critical pedagogy as a way to empower and transform in the classroom and in the communities in which the students reside. This requires conversation, collaboration, and space, both literal and figurative. Tewell reminds us that librarianship is "informed by social justice and activism." In his study of librarians engaged in critical pedagogy, he cites five major benefits of implementing critical pedagogy strategies: they increase engagement; are meaningful for students; are meaningful for librarians; forge connections with faculty; and create community.[1]

One does not need to be in the classroom to practice this. Critical pedagogy has a long reach and can be employed by anyone in the library setting. Here I will focus on the academic librarian in the classroom, by presenting an example of how small, incremental changes can enhance a classroom-learning environment by empowering students to feel valued and safe enough to express their views and opinions in the classroom, and to respectfully challenge and question the opinions and ideas of others.

IT IS WHAT IT DOES

Vangeest and Hawkins prefer to define critical librarianship by how it is *practiced:* by making libraries places of inclusiveness that include people with disabilities; those who do not understand how libraries work; those who do not like to read; and those subject to gender-based, racist, and economic oppression—basically, all the traditionally underserved populations. In the academic library, librarians can help others challenge the institutional racism and gender prejudice that became institutionalized over a long period of time. If a librarian never steps into a classroom, he or she can still enact critical pedagogy at the reference desk and in one-on-one meetings by helping students and other patrons gain access to sources of information they might not have known how to access or did not know even existed. As well, librarians who teach bibliographic instruction or any aspect of information literacy can play an important part in enacting critical pedagogies. According to Sinkinson and Lingold, when we use critical pedagogy in the classroom, information literacy becomes "a potential source of change and empowerment in today's digital world." Per Freire, contexts and topics may change, but "the empowering potential of information literacy will remain . . . a cumulative, developmental process in an individual's life rather than a set of skills to be attained."[2]

AN EXAMPLE OF CRITICAL PEDAGOGY IN THE CLASSROOM

I am the first to arrive at the small computer lab in the ground level of the library. There are twelve students in this particular session of an English 222 class. I watch as they slowly trickle in and scatter across the room, then flop down in front of computers. Soon the room is filled with students who fix their eyes on their computer screens, riveted by Facebook or YouTube. I wait for the professor to come in before I tell them to log on to the university portal and go to the library's homepage. The professor, a distinguished yet laid-back man, comes in with a cup of coffee and sits down in the last row. He gives the class a brief explanation and introduces me. I hear some-one in the back say, not so quietly, "not again," and laughter ripples across the lab. Not yet discouraged, I begin in a fairly standard way, as the professor, Dr. Tom Hemmeter, wanted me to: I do an over-view of the library page with a foray into databases where students might find information on their topics, and then move on to a dis-cussion of their topics.

The professor prods the students good-naturedly, and then, with less patience, chooses one young woman, who appears to be unamused. "I don't know what my topic is yet," she says. She sounds irritated. It will not be until much later in my own process that I will realize that she is not expressing irritation, but rather bafflement. The professor chooses another student, a young man with blond hair tucked behind his ears and a baseball cap slung low over his eyes. The student replies, "James Joyce?" I look to the professor. Predict-ably, he answers: "That is a question. You are supposed to supply an answer." This response elicits some laughter. The professor moves on to a third student, who replies: "I start with Google. I know, that's bad, right? I shouldn't start there. Then I kind of, um, I don't know just put in *Emma* and Jane Austen and manners."

By now, the students are too bored to even be amused by a class-mate's cluelessness. And what is worse, what alarms me, is that they don't even trust their own knowledge. They don't understand that what they are attempting is a process, and that they do not need to have the "right" answer.

My palms are sweaty because I know I have lost them. I have an hour with them and we are 45 minutes in and have barely begun to explore anything of import. I stayed true to my lesson plan and taught everything I thought they needed. But in the end, it wasn't what they needed. I wanted to tell them, like a lover who leaves, "It's not you. *It's me.*"

HOW THIS PROCESS BEGAN

Librarians are constantly challenged to present information literacy in ever more dynamic ways. We add layers of technology, databases, and both creative and tried and true methods like keyword searching. But still we often find it difficult to convince students that what we are there to show them is of any value to them. As I have written in a previous chapter, I have often found that professors or adjuncts in many of the classes we teach are disengaged. In some cases, they use the library session as an opportunity to catch up on their own work, or use the librarian as a substitute teacher for the session. My sessions are usually more productive, and I receive more buy-in from students when professors are engaged in the learning process as *active* rather than *passive* participants. As well, I have dealt with instructors who feel as though they know more than librarians do about their own field (always a frustrating experience), and will interrupt a session with comments or misinformation that lead the session away from its learning objectives. Because students may receive multiple library sessions in different classes, they may tune out most of the information, especially if they consider it to be repetitive. Paradoxically, students often do not absorb all that they should at library sessions because librarians are not always scheduled to meet with them at their exact time of need. Therefore, what we are teaching or presenting in class is often not immediately applicable to their work.

My institution, Arcadia University, is a small liberal arts university with a strong international education mandate located just 25 minutes from Center City, Philadelphia. Serving approximately 4,000 enrolled students, Landman Library employs six faculty librarians, all of whom are engaged in various levels of teaching, from working with first-year seminars and capstone and thesis classes to teaching their own courses according to their specialties. Librarians at Arcadia University enjoy the camaraderie and respect of faculty members on campus; they are involved in many areas of collaboration, from serving on committees to developing and co-teaching courses, although that has not always been the case.

At the time I became a librarian, I had been working as the manager of Access Services at Arcadia's library. I was fortunate to have been offered a faculty librarian position upon completion of my MSLS. I was more than anxious to teach bibliographic instruction. While a staff member, I had heard many of the librarians lament that students do not seem engaged in library instruction classes and rarely, if ever, retain what they are taught. As the liaison to the English department *and* a graduate of both the undergraduate and graduate programs in English at Arcadia, I was treading the line with the professors with whom I worked: they had known me as a student years ago, and now I was their colleague. I had to go slightly off the beaten path to develop the skills needed to connect with the students, while at the same time ensuring that the instruction I was giving would truly propel their research efforts in the right direction. I needed to develop my own way, based on a pedagogy in which I believed. And I needed a class whose topic I felt fluent enough to teach.

ENTER ENGLISH 299

English 299 is a required class for all English majors at Arcadia University. This class prepares students to conduct extended research based on critical theory for their senior theses. They elevate their skills in literary interpretation to a new level as they are introduced to critical theories and learn how to apply them to various texts. Ultimately, the variety of writing projects that the students engage in allows them to synthesize research and theory. The students in this class focus on *Emma* by Jane Austen, *Mrs. Dalloway* by Virginia Woolf, *The Dead* by James Joyce, and *A Midsummer Night's Dream* by William Shakespeare. They are given supplementary handouts on various poems, short stories, and films, as well as on literary theory. They reflect on their reading each week in journals that are collected and graded by the professor. All in all, the goals of this class are to understand theoretical concepts and to apply those concepts to the text with a careful and close reading. In addition, this class begins the process of teaching a more sophisticated level of research writing.

A BETTER WAY

After I conducted a few more sessions in different classes, I felt unsettled about the EN299 session that I had taught, knowing that somehow it could have been much more dynamic. It had lacked energy, and worse, I felt that the students were not any better prepared to conduct research than they had been before my session.

I e-mailed Dr. Hemmeter to suggest another session, one that would build (or tear down and *re-build)* on what we had started. He readily agreed. Two weeks later I walked into the same lab and began by eliciting information from the class before I started doing anything. I asked the stuudents:

- What did you think about our first session?
- How did it help you with your search process?
- What kind of articles did you find that directly related to your topic?
- How will you get to the next step in your research?

The professor required a "zero draft" (one that does not require a structure per se, but only first thoughts or impressions of the topic) before they began writing. Fortunately, this meant I was working with the students early in the process. I went around the room and asked all of them to tell me which text they were focusing on for their first paper, and also describe a bit about their process up to that point. They all told me essentially the same thing: they chose the book they liked best, but were having trouble coming up with a topic. The professor had urged them to pursue ideas that "had legs."

When we finished going around the room, I told the class that unlike the last session, I wanted to make this one interactive and therefore this class would be a workshop. Dr. Hemmeter put down the pen that he had been scribbling with and looked up, and narrowed his eyes a bit. I continued by telling the class that we were a "community of scholars" and that we would be working *together.* I went on to explain this would mean that they would have conversations with themselves and each other, as well as with their professor and me. I discouraged silence in the classroom and cautioned them against getting on the computer right away. "Hands off the keyboards!" I instructed. I disabused them of the idea that their process begins with databases and will end with whatever they find online. I needed to engage them with the material and with one another.

I paired up students who were writing about the same text and asked them to work on conceptualizing their partner's zero draft into possible topics and then viable, searchable words or phrases. The students seemed skeptical at first, perhaps thinking that library sessions should not be interactive at all. Doesn't the librarian just come in and do her thing? At the time, I did not realize that I was creating a new way of teaching bibliographic instruction and that I would be forging a template for how I would teach the class in future semesters, but that is exactly what I was doing.

Because the students needed to interpret their topics through a critical lens and they found theory difficult, we engaged in a bit of role-play. As Dr. Hemmeter portrayed the student and I acted as the professor, we showed them how to begin thinking about their topic and how to approach it by acting out a conversation with each other. The students listened in. It went something like this:

Dr. H: I'm interested in *Mrs. Dalloway*, Professor Reale.

Me: Cool. What about it interests you?

Dr. H: Well, there was the specter of war, everywhere.

Me: That's right. There was.

Dr. H: And that really had to affect Virginia Woolf.

Me: It did. How did you know that?

Dr. H: I didn't, but I am sure it did.

Me: Well, think about Septimus.

Dr. H: Right.

Me: He suffered mental illness that was the cause of his demise.

Dr. H: Exactly. I'd like to know how this affected people at the time.

Me: Good way to think about it, because no one writes in a vacuum. Woolf would have been very affected by the specter of war. I believe she had a brother go off to war.

Dr. H: I want to look into that.

Me: That's a good place to start. You might want to use a New Historicist approach, which would help to understand the book in its historical context.

Dr. H: Ahh! Okay.

SMALL STEPS, BIG CHANGES

It began as simply as that. Verbalizing thoughts and ideas can help to strengthen and clarify them. Much to my satisfaction, the students caught on to how simple those first steps toward their topics could be. Because theory tends to make students squirm and they often think that it is too high-level for them to understand, I asked them to imagine theory as a lens that is slipped over the text that allows it to be seen in a different way. As well, I told them that despite my degrees, and even though I enjoy reading theory, I have to work very hard to understand it. This led to a chorus of sighs and moans about their own experiences with theory. In another context, in another classroom somewhere in time, it might have annoyed an educator to hear students complain about what they don't know. The traditional way of thinking and teaching does not allow for "unknowing," because the goal is mastery of the content. But imagine how liberating it might feel to be able to say in a classroom, "This is tough. I just don't get it." When this happens, safety and acceptance are allowed, along with creative freedom of thought. Students begin to realize that rather than a door closing, one has just opened.

ENTER PAULO FREIRE

As both a librarian and an educator, I am interested in the praxis of critical pedagogy in the classroom. I reject the "banking system" of education, a term coined by Brazilian educator and ideologist Paulo Freire in his groundbreaking book *Pedagogy of the Oppressed*. Freire posits that the traditional way of educating views students as empty vessels just waiting to have knowledge poured into them by a sage, that is, the teacher in the classroom. For me, applying Freire's philosophy and pedagogy in the classroom begins by seeing my students holistically. This means recognizing that they come with thoughts, feelings, perceptions, and many other purely human attributes that influence not only how they learn, but also their capacity to learn, and that I am the "guide on the side" as opposed to the "sage on the stage." This is important, because it helps to empower students to draw on and trust their own thoughts to explore a topic, and then apply rigor to the process. Inspired by Freire, I have them use their own experiences and feelings as they become emotionally involved in the text. Freire believed, and I fully concur, that education and its processes are never neutral. Students need to learn how to find their voices, which liberates them and allows them to fully engage in their own intellectual and educational processes. To me, liberation in the classroom involves taking away the normal constraints of a traditional classroom. For example, the requirement that students must sit and be lectured to (without being allowed to participate) provides them with no opportunity to question themselves and each other aloud. Critical pedagogy raises consciousness; it is hopeful, it is active, and it allows the opportunity to question and critique the subject at hand, and by extension the world at large. When I teach, particularly an EN299 class, I stress that literature is not written in a vacuum, and that they can apply knowledge from their own lives and personal experiences to understand and illuminate texts. And they can do this by working with others. I ask them to dive deep. Then I ask them to surface.[3]

As the librarian embedded in the class, I partner fully with the professor and then partner with the students in a process of "mutualization," whereby my work, the professor's efforts, and the full participation of the class become truly symbiotic. This is in contrast to visiting a class, making a "deposit," and then becoming frustrated and disappointed when the students forget what I told them. It is through this dialogue, this relentless questioning and decentralization of authority in the classroom, that we level the playing field and gently guide the students to form their own conclusions without pushing them toward the answers we have already created.

The academic librarian will discover that teaching presents many challenges. Although one of our mandates is to instruct, we are often limited in our capacity to do so because we are visitors in the classrooms, expected to provide a lesson on skills (though not necessarily to dispense knowledge) to a class that is not really ours. We also may need to negotiate "space" with an instructor or professor who wants us to do the maximum in the minimum amount of time because he or she has more important things on the agenda. I believe that what I have outlined here is not possible in every instruction session, perhaps not even in the majority of them (at least in the beginning). But librarians can make inroads into a different kind of teaching by choosing one subject that they are responsible for and causing a mini-revolution in their approach.

Dr. Hemmeter has expressed to me that the process takes on an entirely new meaning because my sessions are regularly incorporated within his class throughout the semester. He has consistently told me that his students' confidence has increased, both individually and collectively, and that they have improved in all areas of research and its integration. Students tend to express themselves with more ease and become less and less concerned about expressing opinions or making assertions they think may be "wrong" as the semester progresses. Students have even occasionally asked for another class session, and I am always happy to oblige. In each semester of EN299, I do no fewer than three sessions, sometimes more. It is worth mentioning that each session almost always begins with my asking, with an encouraging smile, "Okay. What are we doing and where are we at?" This is certainly a big question, but it is the only prompt that they need before the room is buzzing with conversation. I stand back while my community of scholars gets busy and the real work begins.

FINAL THOUGHTS

There is a plethora of books and articles written on the theory and practice of critical pedagogy. Often, it is difficult to wade through the literature to find a way that is both understandable and adaptable to our own situations in the classroom. In my own experience, I became tangled up in the theory and read nearly everything I could get my hands on, but still struggled to find my entrée into enacting critical pedagogy in the classroom. As I have written before, I believe librarians often focus on too many things in the classroom, leaving students confused and unable to extricate what they can salvage and use. Implementing critical pedagogy strategies in the classroom does not have to fit a textbook description of every possible facet—not by a long shot. What is most important is examining past instruction sessions and identifying areas that cannot only be improved, but may become the change-makers in your classroom. Reflecting on your instruction in different classes will help to reveal distinct aspects of your teaching and how students respond to them, something it is difficult to analyze or consider while you are actively teaching. It is a good idea to look at your instruction practice over time and in many contexts so that you can apply the appropriate strategies to different situations.

We must be mindful of the ways by which we can create spaces and contexts for learning so that we can maximize even the initial small steps toward empowerment. Lankes suggests that you:[4]

- provide access to conversations and materials to enrich conversation
- enhance knowledge creation through direct instruction
- provide an environment conducive to learning
- encourage or build upon the motivation of our members or communities

Establishing a process is more important than gathering every bit of available information, which can backfire and paralyze you. Practice can and should be refined over time as we gather more information and couple it with our experiences in class. The important thing is to take the first step.

Strategies

- Become familiar with the basic tenets of critical pedagogy in both librarianship and in education at large. There is no shortage of literature.

- Your initial steps can and probably should be small. You will change and adjust your practice over time.

- Realize or ensure that you are a *partner* with the professor in the education of his or her students. Recognize, too, that it can be difficult for some professors to allow a shift of power in the classroom if they have not done this before.

- Do not be afraid to go off the program. Often, energy is created in a class when librarians loosen their grip on the agenda and respond to what the students really need (which we can often determine from their questions), rather than what we think they should know. It is much easier to go off the program if you are carefully prepared in the first place. Students possess a wealth of knowledge in so many different areas, although they may not recognize it as such. By allowing them to think out loud, they can more easily conceptualize meaning and make valuable connections within their own thoughts and with others that they would not have made if they were passively sitting and listening. Learning is an activity. We teach students first, material second.

- Pleasantly surprise students by decentralizing the so-called power in the classroom by doing something they won't expect: allow them to take the lead in class discussion and generation of ideas. In the process, they will work out a number of things aloud, so it helps to share some of your own struggles with the research process to build camaraderie and acceptance. For instance, my students are always shocked when I tell them that I struggle with theory despite my master's degree in English. This doesn't lead them to believe that I am not qualified to speak to them about theory; instead they admire and gain confidence from my disclosure that understanding theory takes hard work—and they often feel inspired to exert the same effort.

- Encourage, even in small ways, reflection among the students in class. Although time and frequency of contact are always a problem, I began to employ a strategy that I hoped they would adopt for their own research: when the students are searching databases, ask them to create a search log in which they can list the name of the database they are using, the search terms, and the results. This exercise is twofold: it is metacognitive because it helps them to see their process while they are engaged in it, and it also helps them avoid that awful circular process of throwing search terms into any database to try to come up with something. This helps them to reflect on their process of searching—what works well for them and what does not. Although there are many aspects of reflection, this may be the easiest one to start with.

- Because I have been the librarian in the EN299 class for several semesters, I will often meet with the professor to talk about what we will cover in the class, and I feel comfortable asserting my knowledge of the process as necessary to keep it working. I have not encountered resistance in any semester with this professor and class because, although it was a gamble, what we have done has worked for *this class and this material.*

- Know your discipline and get to know the professor with whom you will be teaching. For instance, I could not work with a biology class as well as I do with English because I do not have the proper language or knowledge of the discipline to to fully engage students in dialogue. But I will learn if I must.

- Reflect on your process. I keep a small notebook and will unobtrusively jot down short notes about my breakthrough moments as they occur. Later, I write comments on how the session went and where I might have done better, what kind of discussions took place, and so on. In one instance this helped me to reflect on how one student in the class came to the aid of another to help her to define her position on feminism and *Who's Afraid of Virginia Woolf.* The student got up from her desk to go and sit with another, who was rather quiet and working alone. In no time at all they were brainstorming together, which gave me the idea of pairing students up during the next session and having them help each other, thus continuing to decentralize the power away from me so that they could share with and benefit from one another.

- Only you can properly communicate to your students and the professor why your role is important. We are our own best advocates, and it is fully in the service of students that we are. It is not that students and professors actively think that we are not an important part of the research process, but rather, it may be that if we are not right in front of them, they may not think about us at all. Take the lead for yourself, for your students, and for our profession.

NOTES

1. Eamon C. Tewell, "The Practice and Promise of Critical Information Literacy: Academic Librarians' Involvement in Critical Library Instruction," *College & Research Libraries* (2017).
2. Jacob Vangeest and Blake Hawkins. "How to Be a #critlib: Reflections on Implementing Critical Theory in Practice," (2016); Caroline Sinkinson and Mary Caton Lingold, "Re-visioning the Library Seminar through a Lens of Critical Pedagogy," *Critical Library Instruction* (2010): 81–88; Paulo Freire, *Pedagogy of the Oppressed* (London: Bloomsbury Publishing, 2000).
3. Freire, *Pedagogy of the Oppressed.*
4. R. David Lankes, *The New Librarianship Field Guide* (Cambridge, MA: MIT Press, 2016).

7

Creating a Welcoming Sense of Place in the Academic Library

Bad libraries build collections, good libraries build
services, great libraries build communities.

—R. DAVID LANKES

Ask any librarian why he or she went into librarianship and
you will find a myriad of reasons, but perhaps one constant:
most of us have loved libraries since childhood. For me the
library was a place of quiet; a place to read; and, shy as I was, a refuge
of sorts. It was also a safe place where I could take part in any number
of activities that were organized for kids, particularly over hot sum-
mers that seemed to last forever. For so many of us, libraries were
places where we not only learned about the world and our interests,
but also learned to become ourselves. There were many places I was
forbidden to go, but the library was never one of them. Although this
view seems nostalgic, and, some might think, plays upon old stereotypes of libraries, it is in fact accurate. But times change, and libraries
change with them. Libraries are no longer monastic places where
one could go and be guaranteed silence—they have now become

social places as well. This is true of public libraries, certainly, but also today's academic libraries.

As an academic librarian, I have despaired at times over the rumors of our own demise and the futility of our efforts to stay relevant. I am also well aware of the controversy over whether or not academic libraries should follow what some consider a public library model of services, where space is taken up with non-library services and where the mythic silence is replaced with programming by students and faculty. Both the social and communal aspects are important to the healthy life of an academic library, particularly if it is small- or medium-sized. Librarians seek to engage more with students, but with the advent of technology, students may not need to ever set foot in the library. This troubles those of us who consider the academic library to be so much more than a repository of information that can be accessed remotely with a few keystrokes, because we know it is a wonderful ecosystem that is vibrant and ever-changing—an all-around great place to be.

COMMUNAL OR SOCIAL?

The future of the academic library has been debated for years, with some having predicted its demise ten or twenty years ago. That we are all still around debating this speaks for itself. I am interested in the more traditional view of the academic library as a place for quiet and focused reading or study (which are largely individual pursuits) as well as the concept that the academic library as a social place where activities and non-library services are offered to the campus community. In the literature, much of the debate favors the more traditional community library, rationalizing that what students and faculty desire most is a quiet place to study, which presumably they cannot find anywhere else. The contention is that all of the other services and activities now populating academic libraries can be found elsewhere, and that they take up valuable real estate and do away with the peace and quiet required for study. Jeffery Gayton believes that "efforts to create a more social academic library threaten this communal spirit, and may do more harm than good." His arguments are compelling, but leave little room to accommodate both the communal and social aspects of an academic library. In this chapter, I would like to explore exactly that issue. Although I fully recognize the reasons behind this argument and acknowledge the dichotomy, I do not think it has to be one or the other, especially in small- to mid-sized academic libraries at teaching (as opposed to research) institutions. In my opinion, Gayton's argument is based on the presumption that the library is a "stand-alone"—that its mission, although undeniably unique and even more undeniably important, is somehow not connected with the rest of the institution, and that its existence is an exception to the larger mission of the university.[1]

THE LIBRARIAN AND THE SOCIAL LIBRARY

There are numerous reasons why some students avoid the library. Library anxiety is a very real phenomenon that has been studied extensively. Students are often unsure of how to use the library (despite numerous and sometimes repetitive bibliographic instruction sessions), or their majors may not require much research. As well, many students can now find most of what they need through library portals, with databases, e-books, and other resources accessible from just about anywhere. Recently, I read an article that called the notion of the library tour a waste of time because students probably would be conducting most of their research online. That kind of thinking—and from a librarian, no less—does more damage to the notion of library as place than any that I have so far seen. We know that students are reluctant library users despite our efforts in the classroom, so planning events and embedding non-library services in the library do something that I think is incredibly valuable: it places students in proximity to librarians and the building itself. Once they are in the library, for whatever reason, they become comfortable with the space and find other reasons to be there. Yes, it is true that no other place on campus can offer the quiet and access to books that a library can, but if seldom used, it becomes a "rarefied" space—rarefied not because it becomes even more desirable, but rarefied in the sense that it becomes less welcoming, and potentially makes students feel as though they are not worthy of it. This is not as far-fetched as it may seem. I have heard more than a few students proclaim that the work that they were doing didn't require peace and quiet, that their work was not rocket science, or that they weren't curing diseases. But libraries are meant to be used, to be occupied, to be vibrant and brimming with possibility. I have always imagined what a difference it would make and how much more influence librarians would have on the lives of students if they were to initially meet and engage them in social activities or other library programs, instead of how we often meet them: when they are stressed and desperate, unable to understand or absorb the help we are trying to give them.

There are many ways to engage with students on our campuses, but when we can embed non-library services or host interesting events (even if they sometimes aren't academic), we reinforce and encourage a sense of belonging. I believe that the library as a social place is becoming increasingly important for students, especially if they are far from home. We have the potential to connect them with one of the most important academic places on campus. Real physical proximity to librarians in the library can reveal to them the many other facets of the library that would otherwise be hidden or inaccessible in a browser window.

In *Libraries as Agencies of Culture*, Augst describes the three ways that libraries function as "place":[2]

- as a social enterprise
- as part of the physical/public infrastructure
- as a place of collective memory

Although some may argue that these characteristics are more suited to the public library, I would argue that the public library is often the first library that students become acquainted with, especially if they attend charter schools or live in districts where school libraries have fallen prey to budget cuts. The community spirit and welcoming nature of public libraries often stand in stark contrast to academic libraries, most of which are intimidating due to their imposing physical structures and the unknowns that come with navigating such a building.

The idea of the academic library as a social enterprise becomes more important in light of these potential student perceptions (or misperceptions). A balance is necessary, but the library must encourage inclusivity (versus exclusivity), even if that exclusivity is only imagined.

PERCEIVING A NEED

Early in my career as an academic librarian, I perceived that our library was important to students for a variety of reasons, and that they saw it as more than a place to study. As the access services and outreach librarian, I am uniquely suited to see students engage in many different activities in the library: those that I employ behind the circulation desk as well as the many other activities and services I have made available in the library through both outreach and on my own initiative.

At my university, there are many first-generation students, as well as students who are far from home and students with disabilities. Our student body is made up of students with these and various other individual and collective characteristics. Students choose a major that interests them and take classes in their field of study that are designed to provide what they will need to be successful. The college experience is not a one-size-fits-all enterprise—students join clubs, play sports, debate intellectually, work campus jobs, and strive to become part of the campus community. Traditionally, the library has stood outside of that experience. My desire was to bring some of those activities to the library, open up the way we interact with students, and revitalize the tired and worn view of the library, so that it would no longer be seen as a boring and stuffy place populated with stern librarians who don't care if anyone is comfortable.

As a person who has always seen the library as a refuge, I understand the importance and potential of what we offer. Everyone is aware of the characterization of the modern academic library as a "warehouse of books" that is seldom patronized; this is discussed, in my humble opinion, in too many futile studies that determine that activities and non-library services do not contribute to the all-important gate counts. With all due respect to these studies (most of which are quantitative), I believe that even a slight shift in services would make a difference. The library can keep its books (of course it can, and should!) while continuing to offer services that will attract students and put them *in proximity* to those valuable resources and the people (librarians!) who have put them there. I do outreach with other academic departments, clubs, and faculty on campus to see how we might be able to fold their services into the library's mission. Truth be told, this has not always been a successful endeavor. I had many ideas that seemed in theory as though they would work, but in practice didn't. But many successful services have been created—some in which I didn't have a hand, others in which I did—that worked out famously and will probably become permanent. It is a matter of trial and error. I have hosted programs that should have been quiet but didn't turn out that way, and others, such as a "gaming day," that should have been lively but were as quiet as could be. So many factors can impact services and programs in the library, sometimes making them successful and sometimes not, sometimes well-attended and other times not—but you won't know until you try.

How do programming and non-library services contribute to how students experience the library as both space and place? They do so by creating a variety of reasons for students to be in the academic library, which in turn contributes to their feelings of being connected to its resources and activities. This helps them to see librarians in traditional and non-traditional roles alike.

For instance, one addition to our library years ago made a huge difference to our student body. I found that I was consistently engaging with students who were voracious readers—of, for instance, science fiction or popular fiction—who would come into the library and quickly find out that they needed to be intentional when looking for something new to read, because the Library of Congress Classification system is not conducive to browsing. Nor did the library have much in the way of leisure fiction, because bestsellers tend not to support the curriculum. This alienated those students for whom recreational reading was a refuge. That was when I decided to subscribe to the McNaughton Leisure Reading Collection, a collection of popular books that is continuously updated by its vendor. I reasoned that because college was a home away from home (both literally and figuratively) for many students, the library could become just like their hometown library by offering popular reading, which is a source of solace in times of loneliness, an excellent de-stressor, and a welcome diversion from their academic studies. It became wildly popular. I have lost count of how many times I have been thanked for adding the collection or how often prospective students touring the library have remarked what a nice addition it is. This was one of the first changes I made in order to create a more welcoming and hospitable environment for students. It is gratifying to see so many students, on any given day, sitting in comfortable chairs reading for pleasure or checking out leisure reading during holidays and spring breaks.

When our new library addition was built in 2003, we had a strict and actively enforced set of rules that I thought were alienating and off-putting; however, it was reasoned that because this part of the building was brand spanking new, all glass, wood, and slate, the goal was to keep it looking new—which, in reality, would have also meant that it looked unused. We spent so much time telling students who came into the library with a soda, a bagged lunch, or a cup of coffee that food was not allowed that we might as well have rolled out the unwelcome mat. It seemed as though people were treating the library as a showpiece or an artifact. The building was beautiful, but buildings, particularly libraries, are meant for use, and it seemed reasonable that students who planned to be in the building for any length of time would want to have food and drink. It did not take a genius to figure out that if students had to pack up all their things in order to get a cup of coffee or have a sandwich, chances are they would not come back. In fact, several focus groups and an extensive survey later, we found this was a reason that people often left the library and why some never bothered to enter. It was an eye-opener and a significant enough result that we not only changed our mission, but expanded it. Any policies that benefit staff but exclude patrons are ludicrous; any that prioritize the maintenance of a building above what our students need seems misguided, or even criminal. While a building itself most definitely contributes to what the campus community, particularly students, perceive as place, it is important to make the space within that place inviting, comfortable, and potentially productive so that it will color students' experiences in a positive way. In their article "Espirit de Place: Maintaining and Designing Library Buildings to Provide Transcendent Spaces," Demas and Scherer note the delicate balance academic libraries should try to create:

> Given the variety of activities that take place in a library,
> one key challenge is achieving a balance among an oppos-
> ing range of functions and needs. Some examples include:
> solitude versus interaction; quiet versus noise; conver-
> sation versus food and drink; order versus mess; exist-
> ing physical barriers versus no barriers; durability versus
> comfort; openness versus security; and limited hours ver-
> sus 24/7 expectations. In addressing these apparent ten-
> sions, it is much too easy to either opt for the status quo
> or succumb to the latest fad and introduce changes for
> the wrong reasons. The successful library meets all of its
> needs through a careful, iterative process of consultation,
> compromise, and design.[3]

This balance is not always easy to achieve, but the effort is worth it.
While campus communities here in the United States and abroad
share many characteristics, each is unique. A one-size-fits-all philosophy may end up fitting a few well, but ignores the needs of all
those on the outside. Librarians and directors are at their best when
they are able to marry what the literature reveals about what works
in libraries with what they learn firsthand from our stakeholders:
students themselves. Focus groups, surveys, and conversations with
students should not only focus on how well our current services are
fulfilling their needs, but also explore what they might like to see
in the library and why. During one focus group, I asked students to
chime in with what they would love to see the library do for or offer
to students—no matter how far-fetched it might seem. Admittedly
the control group was small and the method not entirely scientific,
but I found students to have rather modest wants. Among them
were a café; more movable furniture for collaborative work; hours
extended in both directions (open earlier, close later); better signage;
and the permission or validation that it was okay to use the library
simply as a refuge—maybe as a place to hang out with friends or listen to music on a computer.

There are many opportunities for enhancing library space to
create a sense of place. This list is by no means meant to be exhaustive, and in reality could never be, because innovation is everywhere.
As I am writing this, no doubt there is another innovation ready to

burst upon the scene. A few services that tend to be low-cost and can be evaluated over time are described below.

Services for Students

- writing center
- satellite help desk
- learning enhancement center
- technology lab

Space and Furniture

- study rooms for exclusive student use
- plenty of comfortable furniture near windows
- vending machines for hot and cold drinks and snacks
- movable whiteboards
- tables and chairs that are on wheels for collaborative work
- designated (*and enforced*) quiet or silent areas
- proper signage to make the library easily navigable

Displays

- Arrange attractive and relevant book displays in various places in the library. These should reflect both sides of current issues.
- Feature the books of scholars, writers, and famous alumni and consider hosting a book signing event in the library.
- Set up a wide-screen television to stream breaking news, an election, or an inauguration.
- Liaise with the fine arts department to feature student art in the library.
- Reach out to the community to display the work of local artists.
- Display new books prominently and refresh often.
- Feature recent faculty monographs.
- Consider monthly "staff picks" at or near the circulation desk.

Library Hours

If budget and staffing allow, extend hours to open earlier, close later. Extend hours during midterms and finals.

Coffee and Tea

No suggestion seems to incur the ire of the librarians with whom I have spoken more than this one! Many have told me that the last thing they feel they need to do is to provide coffee and tea for students in lieu of an actual café in their library. And yet, this is one constant in my library that is appreciated more than any other. Throughout the semester, we serve free coffee and tea each Monday, beginning at 9 a.m. This is prepared by the university's Dining Services and is a simple affair that has seemed to go an incredibly long way toward providing an enjoyable visit to the library. Sounds a bit simplistic, doesn't it? It is. It is a welcoming gesture to students, pure and simple. It is especially nice to see students hunker down during cold winter Monday mornings, and once they have their coffee or tea, they more than likely will settle and stay for a while.

Events

Events held in the library should be planned well in advance and be strategic in their value. One of the difficulties in creating "place" in my library was that everyone suddenly wanted to host an event in the library. At first, saying no to many of the requests was difficult, although necessary. To those who were turned down, this may have seemed to be the opposite of what we were trying to do: create a more inclusive place. However, I set criteria that I thought was in line with the mission of our university and was the kind of outreach that aligned with other campus goals and then chose two events per semester.

Communication

The effort to create a library atmosphere that is welcoming to the campus community is all but lost if those efforts are not communicated to the entire campus community. Any event should be publicized well in advance of its occurrence. This can be done in a number of ways, but should always involve online campus calendars, flyers in buildings and dorms across campus, and student mailboxes. Events are likely to have poor turnout if students do not know about them far enough in advance or do not even realize that they are taking place. Although students can be very spontaneous, they are also sufficiently busy that they must plan ahead.

Student Advisory Board

A student advisory board with a librarian as an advisor is a great way to involve stakeholders in decisions about library services. The very nature of a student advisory board is constantly changing, which keeps perspectives and recommendations fresh. As well, student board members are great ambassadors when a library must deny specific requests because of a lack of budget or staffing—they communicate the reasons why and serve as liaisons between library staff and the student population.

Faculty

Last but not least, faculty are more likely to recommend library services to students if they use the library themselves. Particularly on small campuses where space is shrinking or is at a premium, finding space to create a place equipped with appropriate technology for faculty to carry out scholarly work is a great way to support faculty members' own intellectual and scholarly interests as well as their teaching. Make faculty aware of the library's mission to help support their research. Provide space in close proximity to various collections. Our faculty members had expressed the need for space and were grateful for our efforts. Holding a silent writing retreat at least once a semester is another terrific way to show support for faculty. A silent writing retreat is just that—faculty gathered communally to work on a project in silence. The camaraderie of being among colleagues while working decreases the sense of isolation and loneliness that research writing sometimes breeds.

FINAL THOUGHTS

Librarians remain integral in strategizing and implementing ways for our libraries to become places where both the social and intellectual needs of the student are met in safe and welcoming spaces. I have always believed, and in my own practice have seen, that students have a range of motivations to come to the library, just as they check out books for different reasons. I would no more judge the student who checked out a stack of books and never opened a single one than I would someone who comes into the library just to be among others—these are things we could never control, even if we wanted to. And why would we? In other words, although we cannot always know why a student decides to use a library, if we make a welcoming space, they are now in proximity to all that the library has to offer.

Strategies

- Be strategic about changes that you make to enhance the atmosphere of the library. Do this by conducting informal focus groups or campus surveys to elicit information about current services and how students feel about them. It helps to have this kind of baseline information. This also helps you to discover what you are doing right!

- Fads are just that—fads. Resist implementing the latest trend just because it is new and seems cutting-edge or novel. The goal is not to implement change for the sake of change, but to create a set of values around how you would like the campus community to experience the library.

- Involve others in the process. There are many facets to creating a sense of place in the library and others can offer perspective.

- Assess and recalibrate as necessary. If something isn't working out, or your new services lack the necessary consistency, be prepared to make any needed changes.

- See and be seen. I cannot put too fine a point on the difference it makes to truly "see" the students in front of you.

Admittedly, I have days when I am barricaded in my office with a heavy workload—but those are not my best days. Students need to know that we see them, that we are there for them, that we are around: on the floor, in the stacks, and other places. When I am at the circulation desk, I make every effort to greet every single person who walks through the door. It makes a difference!

NOTES

1. Jeffrey T. Gayton, "Academic Libraries: 'Social' or 'Communal'?" The Nature and Future of Academic Libraries," *The Journal of Academic Librarianship* 34, no. 1 (2008): 60–66.
2. Thomas Augst, "Introduction," in *Libraries as Agencies of Culture*, vol. 42, ed. Thomas Augst and Wayne A. Wiegand (Madison, WI: University of Wisconsin Press, 2001).
3. Sam Demas and Jeffrey A. Scherer, "Esprit de Place: Maintaining and Designing Library Buildings to Provide Transcendent Spaces," *American Libraries* 33, no. 4 (2002): 65–68.

8

The Librarian and Reflection

The quality of light by which we scrutinize our lives has direct
bearing upon the product, which we live, and upon the changes,
which we hope to bring about through those lives.

—AUDRE LORDE

We live in an often unbearably busy and noisy world. It
is increasingly difficult, if not impossible, to find quiet
space or time to think. It is no wonder that we have all
but lost the ability to think for and by ourselves given the way we
live now, surrounded by a 24-hour news cycle, phones that have the
ability to do anything and everything, and marketing and advertising
carpet-bombing campaigns that consistently reinforce that nearly
every area of life should be "bigger, faster, stronger." Our students,
too, have become accustomed to receiving constant stimuli, usually in
the form of social media, where they see themselves through the eyes
of others, which Sharon Daloz Parks calls the "tyranny of the they."[1]

Facilitating can be a difficult prospect when students, out of
reflex or fear, reject a process. It seems unbelievably counterintui-
tive: they often may not believe that they have any special insight

into their own thoughts and processes! In addition, although as librarian educators we may understand the value of reflection for ourselves and by extension for our praxis, we may feel that finding the time is too stress-producing in and of itself. The shortage of time in our busy days cannot be denied—and let me say upfront that I understand time constraints as they pertain to my life and the lives of others—but I firmly believe that *not* making the time for some form of reflective practice is a detriment not only to our personal lives but to our professional lives as well.

THE BENEFITS OF REFLECTION

I could write an entire chapter about the benefits of reflection, but for brevity's sake I will say that reflection—an honest and in-depth look at ourselves, our place in the world at large, and how we carry out our work—helps us to connect with ourselves and our everyday teaching practices on a much deeper and more mindful level. This means that we must attempt to stop existing in a thoughtless way, as if we are on autopilot or just going through the motions. It is both a *deliberative* and a *generative* practice. It is deliberative because we consciously choose to cultivate and practice reflection. Usually, this desire comes about because we are experiencing a problem in the workplace, with our students, with the material that we teach, or with something deep within ourselves that leads us to consider changing the way we have been doing things for a long time. Just some of the benefits of reflection for the librarian are:

- increasing our self-awareness
- examining our inner selves
- recommitting our purpose
- challenging preconceived notions
- understanding how we help or hinder ourselves in our lives and our work
- recognizing the possibility of transformation
- becoming proactive in our own lives
- learning from past experiences in order to positively influence future experiences
- revealing our self-imposed limits

- using our insights to help us to live with a vision
- enhancing our ability to focus

Engaging in reflection can and should become a habit of being, particularly for educators. Our active reflective practice benefits not only ourselves, but our students as well. The reason for this is two-fold: when we become more aware of the day-to-day impediments to our praxis or our ways of being with our colleagues, coworkers, and others, we can clarify and change behaviors that do not serve us or those around us. When we teach and practice our profession from a position of inner strength and clarity, including learning or unlearning when necessary, we begin the process of recommitting to ourselves and to our students. The difference will be evident.

GETTING TO A REFLECTIVE MINDSET

Think of an ordinary work day: imagine going through the motions and the types of things that you do every day, starting from the moment you wake up. If you are like me, and I am betting that in one way or another we are all pretty similar, you get out of bed and immediately begin engaging in a routine. Climb out of bed, shower, brush teeth, make something caffeinated to drink, pack a lunch, iron your clothes, and so on. This routine is intensified exponentially if we have school-aged children, pets, or are a caregiver to a spouse, parent, or child. We may do all of these routines while we keep up with the world, by turning on our favorite cable news channel. We may become instantly dismayed at the variety of volatile and tragic situations throughout the world, some of them close to home. We internalize the things we hear without fully understanding how we are affected. We get into our cars and immediately turn on the radio and are either annoyed by loud barking commentary or bombarded by so many commercials that we wonder if we will ever hear a song again. Another radio news channel serves up the same bad news, though in a more thoughtful way, with added editorializing. You drift away, thinking about your morning meeting, the math test your son is going to be taking at 10 a.m., the instruction sessions you have scheduled, your mental grocery list, and then you fret about what to have for dinner.

The distractions that we are subjected to in this day and age are unprecedented and, we are told, harmful to our mental and physical health. We experience difficulty concentrating, focusing, even just being ourselves. We do not know who we are, or how we want to be, because we are constantly being bombarded with outside stimuli from the commercialization of nearly everything, and a brutal and relentless marketing cycle that has us convinced of our lack of worth at every turn. We are either over-committed or under-committed, but the result is usually the same: lack of focus. This is why, very often, the impulse to begin a reflective practice arises from a problem or a need. The impetus is almost always that we cannot sustain ourselves in a healthy way if we go on as we have. What we lack in our lives is a quiet space. Those spaces can either be literal or figurative, but however this absence presents itself in our lives, it is telling us that we must change the way we do things. Time, particularly quiet time, is very hard to find on any given day, and certainly no one is going to give it to you. You must claim it for yourself.

Parks writes of the "power of the pause," an essential space in time that feeds and nurtures both reflective and contemplative practices. She describe this power of the pause thus:

> The moment within the process of imagination that claims our attention here is the essential and widely neglected moment of *pause*. Without the practice of the quality of pause that is integral to the process of imagination and thus to deep learning and human development, we short circuit the kind of transformative learning that is now called for.[2]

In my book on reflective practice for librarians, I reiterate that one of the reasons that reflection and reflective practice is so important for librarians is because it is important for our students, and we must learn that we cannot hold them to any standard of reflection if we are not practitioners ourselves. Not too long ago, I held a faculty workshop on using reflective practice in the classroom. When I polled the faculty members attending the session to learn if any of them used reflection in their classrooms, most of the respondents said that they did. Good enough! But when I then asked how many of them practice reflection themselves, it turned out that very few did, which was puzzling and disappointing. How do you teach something that you yourself do not know? How could or would you possibly evaluate it? What could you genuinely tell your students about its benefits?[3]

If we as librarians are to make a difference in our libraries and with our students, we must have clarity of vision, a clarity that most of us may have once possessed, but which may have become muddy or clouded over time for many of the reasons I've written about earlier in this chapter. So what exactly does the "pause" do for us—how do we benefit? Parks provides clear possibilities for those who engage in reflective practice, exemplified through the essential "pause": "Reflective pauses provide opportunity to consciously return to an earlier experience or insight and seek coherence and meaning—re-patterning an experience or insight that otherwise may unfittingly be incorporated into our habits of life and thought or lost altogether."[4]

"To return to an earlier experience or insight for coherence and meaning" is the very essence of reflection. It often requires sitting with hard truths about our teaching and our very being, and seeking to understand why we experience difficulty in our perceptions and practices. Mezirow calls this a "disorienting dilemma" that has the potential to lead to transformative learning. Personally, I have found this has often been a painful process of stripping away all of the rationalizations that I was using as a shield or the excuses I made when things did not go the way I thought that they should. Of course, a handful of times those excuses and rationalizations were probably warranted—but most of the time they weren't. Yet I plowed through, telling myself that whatever I was doing and whichever way I was doing it had worked so far and it would go on working—until it didn't. I consider myself a naturally reflective person and the times when I used excuses were the times I needed them the most. But whether we are reflective or not, it is in our collective nature to protect ourselves, because admitting that something is wrong means that we must do the hard work to figure out what it is. And when we work it out, we of course must address it and change it, which always feels risky. We fear it will be time-consuming, largely because it is! But finding the time is a must.[5]

MAKING TIME FOR REFLECTION

We make decisions all day long about how we will spend our time. The decision to be reflective necessitates that we make time to do so. Many will react by saying that they could not possibly make time in an already chock-full day. But I say there is always time. Time is, indeed, relative. I remember when I was expecting my second child. Toward the end of nine months I could not, in any way, shape, or form, imagine how I could possibly find the time to bathe, feed, and nurture another child when my days were already a blur of busyness caring for my first-born. But when the second child arrived, though incredibly hairy at first, things fell into place. And I never forgot to take care of either child! Once we make the decision to do something, the way to do it will open naturally.

The old adage "ritual is power; habit is stimulant" could not be truer. What any practice requires of us is that we show up every day. Although it helps to have a regular time and place for reflection, I understand that that is not always feasible; in fact, I do not always find it possible. What is important is that I reflect, in one way or another, every day—but the time and the place may vary. There are many ways to find the needed time. Do not think of the act of reflection as precious or rarefied, or as something that requires loads of time and utter, complete silence. This misconception seems to be the main reason people in our profession are not finding the time to reflect. Make time for reflection, perhaps when you first sit down at your desk in the morning, before you even check your email; when you are sitting outside on your lunch break; or during the last 15 minutes of your day. You can always make bullet points of your thoughts to go back and reflect on later. For some of us, what we write down will be in the form of a question. For example, one that I have used more than once in the past (and probably will in the future!) is "How was my teaching affected today by the fact that the class showed no enthusiasm whatsoever?" Sometimes I have reacted with anger or exasperation. On other occasions, I felt somewhat hopeless and felt that what I was doing and how I was doing it were not respected, and that what I was doing did not matter in the long run. Reflecting on this has been particularly helpful because as I examine my feelings from all sides I acknowledge that although I'd had a bad session, the majority of my sessions were not like that. But what was it about that specific session, on that particular day? I will often begin with a question and then strip away all illusions and projections.

JOURNALING

Reflection is often uncomfortable and embarrassing. It can also be extremely revelatory, in that there is no point in lying to ourselves— no one will see what we write in our reflective journals. To transform, to move out of a stuck spot, and to gain new insight, we need to know why we are where we are.

Keeping a reflective journal is essential to good reflective practice. It is interesting how many people turn up their noses at the thought of keeping a journal. One colleague spoke of his distaste for "diary-keeping." Others have told me that they don't like to write, that journaling would feel unnatural, and that they would rather reflect in their heads (presuming they wanted to reflect at all). Yet others feel that there is no special art to it, and that because we are constantly thinking about the things that we do, we are always reflecting. Well, that is true, to a point. We are always thinking of the things that we are doing: sometimes while we are actively doing them and sometimes, usually with remorse, after they are done. But what happens during those times? I can ruminate until I can't ruminate any more, but that will not change the outcome of what has already occurred. In time, I will forget the unfortunate or uncomfortable incident until a similar incident arises and I once again begin another, often self-recriminating, rumination. Reflection that occurs only within my mind is doomed to stay there. There will likely be no action, no real examination that is not distorted by my self-judgement, and no chance for transformation. When we commit our thoughts and feelings to paper, we are engaging in a deliberate and transformative practice. We write what we feel, look at what we wrote, and sit with it. What we write is often more revelatory than what we merely think. Writing something down on paper is a commitment of sorts, because it puts the problem in a tangible form that is more real than some of our own thoughts, which can become nebulous over time if not written down.

Mankey believes that journaling can help us feel more comfortable in unmasking our humanness. She highlights that one of the benefits of keeping a reflective journal "is that we can read our entries to see patterns of behavior or thinking" and that "when we see patterns, we can develop a heightened awareness of how and when our humanness is likely to manifest so we can reflect in action." Further, Mankey emphasizes that another byproduct of establishing a reflective practice is that it allows us to become proactive instead of remaining in the reactive state in which most of us exist.[6]

JOURNALING TECHNIQUES

There are a variety of ways to keep a reflective journal. In my book *Becoming a Reflective Librarian and Teacher: Strategies for Mindful Academic Practice*, I list several techniques for reflective journaling:[7]

Stream of Consciousness or Free Writing

This strategy is one that many who are new to reflective writing feel most comfortable with: a spontaneous and "clearing-of-the-throat" type of writing in which you just begin writing whatever you are preoccupied with at the moment, exactly the way you are thinking it. This is not polished or planned writing, nor is it meant to be. Free writing is essentially the same process, though with free writing you may decide to give yourself a topic and then just write to that topic. For instance, you could choose "How do I feel when students show up to class totally unprepared?" You can either use stream of consciousness or free writing. There are no rules, nor should there be! The goal is to get your thoughts and feelings down on the page so that you can begin to find clarity on the situation, which may lead to a new way of solving the problem that then leads to transformation.

Dialogue

Using dialogue as a strategy in reflective writing means that you have a conversation on paper which you start with a question and then proceed to answer—though be warned it will not be "the" answer, but rather the first steps in figuring things out. Clarity often comes with time and with the habit of writing. While we are seeking answers, we must acknowledge that the process itself is of the utmost importance. Dialogue shows us that.

Lists

Generating lists using bullet points or a numbering system is an effective way to get your thoughts down on the page when you do not have the time or energy to engage in narrative thought or writing. The ease with which we can create a list and the immediate relief that we often feel in being able to capture our thoughts so quickly makes this strategy a welcome one for those who genuinely have difficulty finding time for reflection during the workday. You can go back to your list(s) in the evening or the next day and expound on what you jotted down. This is the generative aspect of reflective writing, because now, when you open your notebook, you already have a place to begin!

Drawing

Drawing is a great way to reflect. Instead of words, which often tire us, we can simply sketch something on the page. Many artists, and even writers, have used drawing as a way of releasing tension, identifying their feelings, and solving problems. You do not have to be a trained artist to draw in a sketchbook: you only need the desire to do so. Occasionally, I will sketch in my journal when I feel too fatigued to put my emotions into words. One particular entry into my journal was a drawing of black and blue spirals with varying degrees of thickness in the lines. I didn't think, but just felt my way through. It had been a bad day, full of what seemed like non-stop misunderstandings with colleagues and students, and the sketch was all I could come up with. A day later, feeling better after a good and desperately needed night's sleep, I looked at that journal entry with a keen insight that I had not had the day before. I noted the colors I used (I was feeling a bit beat up, thus black and blue) and the shapes I concocted (downward spirals). Only 24 hours before, I felt pretty lousy about myself. My journal entry reminded me of that, but also reminded me that I could (and did!) overcome that feeling. If I feel like that again (and it is certain that I will), that journal entry will serve as a reminder that I can survive a tumultuous day.

Poetry

Again, the only rule is that there are no rules. You do not need to be a trained poet in order to create poetry in your journal. Poetry is distilled thought, often using figurative language. Perhaps you feel trapped, like a bird? Perhaps childlike, because your boss treats you that way? Invisible, because your students don't see you? All of these feelings and then some can be expressed by a few words on each line. Haiku is a wonderful entrée into writing poetry to express a feeling evocatively. The basic form of the haiku is 5–7–5, which indicates the number of syllables on each line. The form influences content, requiring us to be short and to the point. Here is an example of a haiku that I wrote after feeling invisible to a class full of brand-new first-years:

> The faces looked at
> me like empty signs saying
> nothing, just a stare.

Metaphor

Use metaphor to express how you feel by comparing your feelings to something similar. Perhaps you're so stressed you feel as though you are in a straightjacket; your office is so dirty that it would need the Environmental Protection Agency to clean it up; your coworker's complaining is so pervasive that you feel as though you are stuck in rising flood waters. The fact is, we live in metaphor and we use it to express ourselves all the time. When we bemoan a separation from those we love, we might say we are heartbroken or that our heart has split in two—although, of course, we know that that is literally not possible. Still, humans have found various and sundry ways to express how we feel. Metaphors help us to see things in different ways, and a change of perspective is often exactly what we need. According to Stevens and Cooper, metaphor can be used in our professional lives to yield the following advantages:[8]

- to better understand your organization or yourself as a professional
- to understand different perspectives about a project
- to develop creative responses to challenging problems at work
- to look at something from another point of view

Using metaphor in our reflective journals will provide a new way of seeing, which, in turn, will open up new perspectives and new ways of solving our problems.

Narrative

Narrative is my preferred form of journaling. I feel the most comforted when I can use narrative to tell a story. I set a context and then proceed (sometimes with blow-by-blow description) as objectively as I can—I may not succeed completely, but I try. Although my writing is very personal and specific to my own situation, narrative often affords me a view from a distance. This perspective comes after the fact, because while I am writing, I am able to see details more clearly than when I was in the midst of the action. Narrative writing is evocative and stirs up an emotional response. I like to note specific details—the smell of the classroom, the way a slant of light fell across my computer screen, the absolute silence when I asked a question, and how I felt as the seconds ticked by while I waited for a response. All of these evocative details are clues to how a certain experience affected me, which gives further insight into a situation. It is storytelling at its best—not fictional, but real. We live storied lives and we tell stories all the time. Try to remember the last story you told: how it had a beginning, a middle, and an end; how you colored it with details to entertain but also to recreate the scene as closely as possible. A story of a family feud at a wedding that merely says that Uncle Fred and Aunt Mary got into it again tells us that there was conflict, but not why or how. But if I know that Aunt Mary split her gold lamé dress down the side as she was leaning over to pick up her purse from the floor when she left in a huff because Uncle Fred was drunk again and making goo-goo eyes at cousin Bill's new girlfriend, *that* I can understand. Aunt Mary must not only have been furious at Uncle Bill's embarrassing flirtation, but mortified that she tore her tasteless, though expensive, dress. An incident or problem need not be funny or dramatic, but it will be full of details. It is your duty, and will be to your benefit later, to record these—they are touchstones that will help you to remember how you were feeling and what influenced those particular emotions.

FINAL THOUGHTS

Reflection is a worthwhile practice that strengthens our personal and professional selves by increasing our awareness and understanding of all parts of our lives. It is a deliberate and intentional practice; a proactive path to self-actualization; the ability to communicate our needs and frustrations in a productive and respectful way; a means to more fully understand the organization in which we work; and to develop compassion for others who are, undoubtedly, encountering the same issues. Mankey astutely asserts: "meeting ourselves where we are and realizing that what we can control lies within us is directly and immediately applicable to our work with students." And in the end, that is what it is really all about![9]

Strategies

- Resist the urge to overthink reflection. There is no need to over-intellectualize or fret about it. It is important simply to begin.

- Consider the journal that you will write in: choose one that you will look forward to using. Bookstores carry an array of delicious blank journals just waiting to be written in. Your reflection deserves a decent home.

- Try to find time to journal each day, if only to write a few words. Reflective practice benefits from regularity. The more you "show up," the easier the writing becomes and the more revelatory the passages that you write will be.

- Allow yourself to engage in a variety of techniques. Don't let this intimidate you. Remember, this reflective journal is for your eyes only.

- Writing rituals can enhance reflective writing. Lighting a scented candle, listening to classical music, or working in your favorite coffee shop can set just the right mood to help you write—which, of course, will beget more writing.

- Often, while in the throes of a dilemma, we find it difficult to put into words exactly what we are feeling. If this is the case, start with a statement or a question. For instance, ask "How do I feel when the professor does not help to keep the students quiet during my presentation?" or "I hate to be asked to teach a class at the last minute, it makes me feel . . ." Give yourself permission to begin with only a statement or questions. Then write about that statement or question, or respond to it with a drawing, a poem, or any of the other journaling techniques listed on the previous pages.

- Revisit what you have written. When you have filled enough pages, you will be able to discern patterns in your responses to things that upset you, throw your teaching off kilter, or prevent you from getting along with a colleague who has a different teaching philosophy. As well, you will see an emerging pattern of insights that will guide you toward resolution and transformation.

• Work deliberately to give yourself reflection time and then to protect it. We must make time; it is not given to us. In the end, we all get the same 24 hours a day, and so much of that time is wasted. Better to be reflecting than wasting time.

• Remind yourself constantly that reflection and establishing a reflective practice are signs of healthy professional self-esteem. Far from being an add-on or an afterthought, reflection can be our anchor, the cornerstone of our personal and professional lives that, with a bit of effort, can truly transform us as well as those around us.

NOTES

1. Sharon Daloz Parks, *Big Questions, Worthy Dreams: Mentoring Young Adults in their Search for Meaning, Purpose, and Faith* (San Francisco: Jossey-Bass, 2000).

2. Sharon Daloz Parks, "The Power of the Pause in the Process of Human Development," in *Contemplative Approaches to Sustainability in Higher Education: Theory and Practice*, ed. Sharon Daloz Parks, Marie Eaton, Holly Hughes, and Jean MacGregor (New York: Taylor & Francis, 2016).

3. Michelle Reale, *Becoming a Reflective Librarian and Teacher: Strategies for Mindful Academic Practice* (Chicago: ALA Editions, 2017).

4. Parks, "The Power of the Pause in the Process of Human Development, 23.

5. Parks, "The Power of the Pause in the Process of Human Development"; Jack Mezirow, *Fostering Critical Reflection in Adulthood: A Guide to Transformation and Emancipatory Learning* (San Francisco, CA: Jossey-Bass, 1990).

6. Richard C. Mankey, "Dialogue, Reflection, and Learning: From Our Spiritual Center," in *Reflection in Action: A Guidebook for Student Affairs Professionals and Teaching Faculty*, ed. Kimberly Kline and Edward P. St. John, (Sterling, VA: Stylus Publishing, 2014).

7. Reale, *Becoming a Reflective Librarian and Teacher*, 55–67.

8. Joanna E. Cooper and Dannelle D. Stevens, "Journal-Keeping and Academic Work: Four Cases of Higher Education Professionals," *Reflective Practice* 7, no. 3 (2006), 349–66.

9. Mankey, "Dialogue, Reflection, and Learning," 90.

9

Librarians as Leaders

A leader is one who knows the way,
goes the way and shows the way.

—JOHN C. MAXWELL

t is neither unique nor new to pose the question, "what makes a leader?" At the outset, let me say that I fully recognize this. I would also like to add that the answers to that question are often delivered in bullet points, most of which involve the words *power*, *integrity*, or *influence*. Having read so much in my career about what it means to be a leader left me feeling like those articles and books were written for someone else, certainly not me—and not because I did not see myself as a leader, or because I did not think myself capable of wielding power over others—far from it. I did not feel then, nor do I now, that being a leader means having power over others as much as it means enacting my own ongoing professional development so that I can set high standards for myself and be in a position to help others do the same. We live in an age where leadership has both a cult status and a cult following. The first minutes of any news broadcast will start off reporting on those who are "in charge" (and not necessarily for the better).

Few people outside of our field think of librarians as leaders. That is a pity, because I think that librarians are perfectly positioned for many different kinds of leadership. Sasso and Nolfi note that academic librarians' roles change out of necessity, and explain that "academic librarians are innovative problem solvers, experts at working within financial, space, and time constraints, and skilled at collaborating in cross-disciplinary teams and working with diverse populations." Further, they assert that the volume of changes in the academic librarianship within a relatively short period of time "prepares us to adapt to the challenges of leadership at the institutional level." I would, of course, agree. Although there are many approaches to the path of leadership, I believe that academic librarians are already enacting leadership in our efforts toward greater collaboration on our campuses, whether via work with faculty, embedded librarianship, liaison librarianship, information literacy plans, institutional repositories, copyright education, or a host of other activities. I am interested in the many facets of leadership that involve not only campus initiatives (which remain the most visible examples of leadership), but also those situations that help librarians, whether or not they have taken on extra or expanded roles on campus, enact leadership—what I call the "leading from wherever you are" school of leadership.[1]

LEADERSHIP'S MANY FACES

Interestingly, the concept of leadership varies from person to person and from organization to organization. Academic libraries across North America structure their organizations in different ways. Some use a quasi-shared sort of governance; others have directors or deans or are led by head librarians; some are partnered with Information Technology, in which case a CIO may be in charge of the blended department. Although it is important to recognize the differences in these structures of leadership, oftentimes the exclusive focus is on who is appointed to be in charge, thereby totally overlooking less stereotypical instances of leadership that occur every day in academic libraries.

A few months ago, my boss alerted me to an article that I found incredibly enlightening—so much so that I read it several times and then saved it. In his article "Leading from All Sides," Joseph Janes writes of those who "lead from the middle," a group that in reality includes more members than those who are officially appointed to sanctioned leadership positions. I had never thought of what my colleagues and I did as "leading from the middle," but in essence that is exactly what we do. Janes offers what he calls an "alternative idea" that turns the idea of traditional leadership on its head: he suggests that we can, and often do, lead from right where we are, even though what we do might not be recognized as leadership per se. But, of course, it should be.[2]

Janes emphasizes that leading from the middle is more than just showing up, more than just being a good committee member. He clarifies his stance by asserting that a person who leads from the middle is

> guiding, and shaping, moving things forward, articulating a vision and marshaling support for it, creating and innovating, doing something that likely otherwise would not have been done. And from the ranks, without the benefit of—or need for—a title or position from which to accomplish that. It's not necessarily subversive or diversionary, but it's tricky since you don't have the benefit of the machinery of office to turn your ideas into reality.[3]

This type of leadership would seem to take personal ego out of the equation because you may or may not get credit for initiatives. However, I suspect that those who find themselves leading from this position are not particularly concerned about this in the first place. It requires an emotional intelligence, and what Janes describes as the skill to "persuade and sway, rather than cudgel or mandate."[4]

To lead from the middle, then, requires that librarians not only enjoy what they do and that they "show up," both literally and figuratively, but must also be aware of the influence that they have within their organizations and be mindful of the responsibilities that come with influence.

Years ago, before I came to the library where I am now the access services librarian, I worked in a busy public library system where outside experts were brought in frequently to present cutting-edge security training. Having always worked in circulation, I knew in a deep and visceral way that public spaces, wonderful as they are, can also be places where individuals can wreak havoc if they so desire. At the time of the tragic and senseless Columbine shootings, those of us who worked in public spaces had a very real wake-up call, and the system that I worked for responded. I felt well-trained and mindful, and my awareness of my surroundings was raised to a whole new level.

When I moved to a university library on a small campus, I was stunned at the lack of security measures and training for those working in what was then a brand-new addition to the library building. It was large and cavernous—and therefore a difficult place in which to feel secure. I had no real standing whatsoever upon my arrival because not only was I a new employee, but was then a paraprofessional. I managed the circulation desk—a low-level position that seemed to pale in importance to other roles in the library. I may not have been in a position of power, but I took my job quite seriously. My concerns about security mostly fell upon well-meaning but deaf ears, because at that time the library's leadership was in flux and it was preparing to merge with Information Technology (a plan that, incidentally, failed). I began making lists of security concerns in the library, focusing on the building, the hours of operation, the many people who had access to the building after hours, and the fact that many of the work-study students that we employed lacked any kind of training in safety. Because I had never been employed in an academic library setting, I read whatever I could get my hands on concerning safety procedures and best practices in academic library spaces.

I began to document incidents, including several where local police needed to be called and two people were banned from the library. I questioned things that, from a safety and service viewpoint, did not make sense to me. For instance, why were the five unnetworked computers meant for visitors located on the lower level, a place my student workers were fearful of venturing into after 5 p.m.? I continued to document issues and write up recommendations for quite some time, then compiled them into a document. I added a top sheet of bullet points that highlighted what I considered the most pressing issues regarding safety and security in the library. All along I'd been told that what I was doing was a waste of time, and that my efforts would likely be ignored and unappreciated. I was not deterred, in part because I believed that massive changes needed to be made and I saw that I was the only one who knew enough to make them happen. I would have said that I was leading from the middle, but now as I write these words I see that, far from leading from the middle, I was enacting leadership from the periphery! I suppose I was what Robert E. Kelley would call "an effective follower." I followed in the sense that I was not in charge overall, but rather was proactive in my small area. According to Kelley, there is one overarching quality of the effective follower: the ability (and the desire) to be proactive and exert great effort to accomplish a greater common purpose.[5]

THE MYTH OF POSITION

John C. Maxwell, a a well-known author who writes about leadership, calls for "leadership in every direction," which involves leading up and across, reaching even to those above you. He explains that "99 percent of all leadership occurs not from the top but from the middle of an organization." Maxwell is not speaking specifically about libraries, but his words are relevant because the structure of most academic libraries is very similar to those of many other industries. Most organizations battle what Maxwell calls the "myth of leading from the middle of an organization," which may be particularly true in academic libraries where there are often clearly drawn lines between paraprofessionals, librarians, and directors. You may recognize some of the myths that may have prevented you from thinking of yourself as a leader.[6]

1. **The Position Myth—I can't lead if I am not at the top.** This thinking is pervasive. The bold truth is that you can make a difference, big or small, from any position within an organization.

2. **The Destination Myth—When I get to the top I will learn to lead.** We learn as we go along, every single day.

3. **The Influence MythIf—I were on top, people would follow me.** Think of how much resistance the person at the top often meets. People follow those who they respect and can trust.

4. **The Inexperience Myth—When I get to the top I will be in control.** Complete control at the top is another myth. Everyone has a boss to whom they are accountable.

5. **The Freedom Myth—When I get to the top I will no longer be limited.** Every position of power has limits. Responsibility increases with leadership positions, inherently limiting our power.

6. **The Potential Myth—I can't reach my potential if I am not at the top.** We have the potential to be effective and dynamic wherever we find ourselves on the organizational ladder. Working to our fullest potential is one of the most important goals we can strive for.

7. **The All or Nothing Myth—If I can't get to the top, then I won't try to lead.** If we do not lead from where we are, we will seldom if ever go beyond our daily mandate, in effect cutting off our chances of being considered for a leadership position!

Leaders do not take these myths to heart. Doing so would be counterproductive to any form of leadership. The idea that if we want to effect change, anywhere is better than where we already are could not be farther from the truth. We *can* and *should* lead from where we are.

Pixey Anne Mosley, a professor and associate dean for administrative and faculty services at the Texas A&M University Libraries, states that "an organization's overall success is going to be dependent on the commitment, engagement, and culture found at levels well removed from the administrative suite and this sort of peer-based leadership development may be what is more critically needed within organizational cultures to build grassroots leadership and move libraries forward."[7]

Each library has a culture that influences how its staff responds to challenges: either proactively, or reactively with great resistance and fear of change. One could surmise that the best way to not only survive but thrive in the library work environment would be to embrace change, which is an undeniable and unstoppable condition of libraries everywhere. The old adage, "change is the only constant," is as true a statement as ever uttered regarding libraries. It requires, among other qualities, great flexibility and forward thinking from those individuals who work within their walls.

SOME LEADERSHIP CHARACTERISTICS

Listening

It can be a demoralizing experience to find yourself communicating with a boss or supervisor who is tone-deaf to your thoughts or opinions—worse still, one who sees leadership as a title instead of a role, for whom every change or initiative comes from the top down. That is not leadership—that is dictatorship. One of the most basic core values of librarianship is that of listening, truly listening, to the needs of our students or patrons to be able to provide the information they are looking for, and also to provide a satisfying experience. This entails that we be mindful of the person in front of us. Often, core values do not translate to leadership in libraries, but they should. Mosley considers the ability and willingness to listen in a "thoughtful and engaged way" a core characteristic of leadership:

> This does not mean that one can automatically dismiss or ignore the barrier of an initial emotional response in order to engage, but it does mean that once a person has had a change to present their view they must be willing to listen and consider the other perspective and be willing to seek a mutually satisfactory solution. This requires that the titled leadership also demonstrate leadership skills of listening and willing to change perspective rather than being defensive to having one's ideas challenged. Part of leadership is choosing the appropriate leadership behavior within context of a particular situation or circumstance.[8]

Situations in which people are heard and respected help to foster healthy work environments. There will always be days when things go wrong, where someone disagrees with us at a staff meeting, our proposals are turned down, or we feel as though our work is not valued—this is a fact of life in every work environment, and contrary to popular belief (usually held by people who know little or nothing about libraries), libraries are often high-powered, competitive, and contentious spaces. But I can hardly think of a scenario that a caring and intelligent leader could not help to alleviate the tension by actively listening to someone's concerns and offering support and encouragement.

Hopefully we have seen, or soon will see, the end of those days when we are forced to suck it up and ignore our feelings about issues at work in order to conform to some notion of pseudo-professionalism. Not being heard is harmful not only to our psyches, but also to our workplaces. We bring our whole selves to our profession, not just select parts that we polish up for public consumption. We are real people, battling all sorts of problems that we often have no control over during the workday. But how much better would it be for all of us if we were viewed holistically by those in leadership positions who are also willing to listen to us in attentive and caring ways?

Shared Goals

Facilitating shared goals or a unified vision is essential to library leadership. Often people will resist change because they have been either kept in the dark until a change is announced, or they have known that change was coming but were totally marginalized and thus forced to watch from the sidelines instead of participating. Libraries are not corporations. Good library leaders will develop shared goals with staff so that everyone has a sense of purpose and understands that achieving a goal will require effort from all. It also gives people the opportunity to excel in their particular areas of expertise, or to develop a new area of interest. Being able to express these desires is important, as is coming to agreement about what the desired goals and outcomes are.

Mistakes as Opportunities for Growth

Leaders who not only recognize that anyone who hopes to grow professionally will make mistakes and who will tolerate those mistakes to encourage further growth are worth their weight in gold. In my early days of academic librarianship, I pushed the envelope with a few ideas that resulted in unforeseen failures and complications. Sometimes I spoke up at meetings out of an intense desire to make my mark when I would have done better to just listen, and sometimes I was passive, when it would have been in my best interest to act. At that time, I had weekly meetings with my boss, a wise and careful listener who would encourage me to talk about my concerns. In one case, I had been working with a professor who had judged me rather harshly because he thought I had given bad information to one of his students. I only found out about this when he told a colleague that he didn't want to work with me. I vented about this one day in a meeting with my boss, who just listened. When I came to the end of my story, and explained I thought I'd been unfairly (not to mention incorrectly) characterized, she asked me how I planned to resolve the issue, "Because," she added, "It *must* be resolved." I told her I didn't know what to do—that I felt ashamed and dreaded any other contact or interaction with this professor. She reassured me that my mistake—if in fact it was a mistake—was acceptable, and told me that misunderstandings will happen, and that I would have to face my fear of dealing with the situation. I realized two things: first, that I was so deeply ashamed about what happened that I had only told my boss about it because I was afraid she would hear about it from someone else, and second, that I didn't think I was allowed to be wrong. The first assumption made sense—my boss might have heard it from someone else down the line, but the second was incorrect. I was allowed to be wrong. I was allowed to make mistakes. Her expert mentorship and guidance helped me to correct my mistakes, but also showed me that taking chances was essential to my professional growth, even if this meant that I might fail.

Honoring Different Styles

The recognition that leadership is found at every level of a library organization is an important one. Understanding this allows us to identify initiative and innovation when we see it. We expect those who have the propensity for leadership to look and act a certain way: usually "dressed for success," confident—sometimes overly so, and with just a tinge of enough arrogance to inspire confidence (or fear) in others. And maybe that is how leadership looks in places such as big corporations, but it doesn't usually present itself that way in academic libraries. Mosley notes that librarians are, traditionally, "conflict averse," which results in a preoccupation with getting along with everyone. This in turn results in the inability to detect leadership qualities in those who are too "passionate" or "assertive." The former quality could be seen as being too emotional, the latter as too aggressive. Instead of relying on stereotypical personality types, leaders should look for *qualities* of leadership, even if they present themselves in very different ways than in our preconceptions or preferences.[9]

FINAL THOUGHTS

Leadership is a characteristic, not a title. It is an active way of being—how we carry out our individual duties, and how those efforts contribute to the smooth running of our libraries and the overall health of our organizations. Leadership, no matter how it presents itself, will prioritize the organization over aggrandizement of self. Everyone possesses leadership qualities—and a good leader, no matter where he or she sits, can recognize and reward those efforts.

Strategies

- Avail yourself of opportunities for professional development, not only in your particular area of expertise but also in those that build leadership skills.
- Clearly communicate your desire for leadership opportunities to your boss or supervisor.
- Seek a mentor. Some people may be born leaders, but many, if not most, have learned at the elbows of other leaders.
- As you develop leadership qualities in yourself, look around and recognize and encourage them in others.
- Realize that opportunities for leadership are everywhere.
- Be humble. Being a leader doesn't mean that we know everything. Recognize that learning can, does, and must occur at every level, even at the top.
- Take the words of John C. Maxwell to heart: "Leadership is a choice you make, not a place you sit."[10]

NOTES

1. Maureen Diana Sasso and David A. Nolfi, "Librarians as Academic Leaders: Uniquely Qualified for the Job." In *Sailing into the Future: Charting Our Destiny*, Proceedings of the Thirteenth National Conference of the Association of College and Research Libraries, March 29–April 1, 2007, Baltimore, Maryland (Chicago: American Library Association, 2007), 325.
2. Joseph Janes, "Leading from All Sides," *American Libraries* (March/April 2014).
3. Ibid.
4. Ibid.
5. Robert E. Kelley, "In Praise of Followers," *Harvard Business Review Case Services*, 1988.
6. John C. Maxwell, *The 360 Degree Leader: Developing Your Influence from Anywhere in the Organization, Workbook Edition* (Nashville, TN: Thomas Nelson, 2006).
7. Pixey Anne Mosley, "Leadership Writ Large, Beyond the Title." *Library Leadership & Management* 28, no. 2 (2014).
8. Ibid., 4.
9. Ibid.
10. John C. Maxwell, *The 360 Degree Leader: Developing Your Influence from Anywhere in the Organization* (Nashville, TN: Thomas Nelson, 2011).

10

On Being Indispensable

I have come to believe that caring for myself
is not self-indulgent; caring for myself is survival.

—AUDRE LORDE

Being or becoming an indispensable librarian is a wonderful thing—for the most part. But librarians who work in an ever and rapidly changing environment (which means nearly all of us) are subject to the stresses of work just like everyone else because so much of what we do—especially those of us who also teach—involves interaction. Stress can be compounded by increasingly heavy workloads, shrinking staff, and the pressure not only to perform our jobs each day but also to keep up with the many changes that occur so frequently in our profession. Taking care of ourselves is essential to preventing what we most dread—burnout.

A common perception of libraries, and by extension library work, is that they are non- or low-conflict environments, and that library work is peaceful. We know this is not true, but people are not easily convinced! Others do not understand what we do and believe that whatever it is we do is not difficult, and therefore certainly not stressful. I remember not too long ago buying a train ticket into Center City, Philadelphia, and having the older gentleman behind me ask what I did for a living. "Librarian," I said with a smile that expressed how proud and happy I was to be doing work that I love. "Huh," he said, an index finger poking behind the thick eyeglass lens of his right eye. "Interesting. But what do you do when you're not stamping the books?"

NIP STRESS IN THE BUD

As I write this, I fully understand that what I am about to propose is easier said than done. In our line of work, it is absolutely essential that we take care of mind, body, and spirit. When we encounter stressful situations (which, according to the law of averages, is inevitable), feeling healthy and happy will go a long way to alleviate the havoc that stress is just waiting to inflict. This is especially important for those of us who have not been practicing self-care. If we are emotionally run down or physically exhausted, things that normally would not even appear on our radar will begin to keep us awake at night. Not only have I been there myself, but I have seen this happen to friends and colleagues. Whole books have been written about the subject! There are a variety of ways we can begin to care for ourselves both in and out of the workplace. Often at work I feel so pressured that I just don't have time to think, which means I become reactive to situations because of a real or perceived sense of stress or duress. I have implemented a variety of strategies that have helped me to cleanse my emotions, learn to stay in the moment, and prevent me (well, most of the time) from reacting to everything around me. Among them:

Unplug

Shut your devices off. This seems obvious, but so many of us have trouble doing so. If you must check your email after work, designate a time. Check it once and then shut it down for the rest of the night.

Reduce the amount of time you spend engaging in social media.
I used to have a Twitter account until I realized that the level
of snark and nasty cleverness I found there was just too much
—and totally irrelevant to my life. . It didn't add anything to
my experience of life, so I deactivated my account.

Uninstall Facebook Messenger from your phone. Even if you
are not using Facebook, your phone will ping each time
someone sends you a message. If you are like me, you are
almost Pavlovian in your response to that sound: *It must be
important! Let me just check it for one minute!* If it is important,
there are other ways to reach you. Checking it is a time suck
and a waste when you could be doing something enjoyable.

Emails do not need to be responded to immediately. In fact, no
one expects you to. A wise boss told me this in response to
my constant and almost compulsive habit of monitoring my
email so that I could answer in record time. That kind of
thinking just feeds on itself, and you become a slave to it.
And, as we all know, the emails will never stop coming, so
it is better to deal with them in batches several times a day,
rather than constantly monitoring them.

Spend your time wisely

Don't overcommit. It almost feels cliché to even write this. So
many in our profession regularly disregard this simple piece
of sage advice. We are committed up to our eyebrows. We
already have so much on our plates without piling on more.
And yet, we do.

**If you are constantly being asked to do even more than you
already are, at least slow down and evaluate what is being
asked of you.** Ask yourself: Do I really have time for this?
Will this enhance my skill/knowledge/satisfaction? Am I just
saying yes because I am afraid to say no? While we won't be
able to decline all we're asked, many requests can and should
be evaluated more critically.

Resist the urge to answer immediately. There are rarely emergency requests in the library. When asked to do something that will impinge on our personal lives or will take a physical or emotional toll, we may end up blabbering out a string of excuses and then feel stressed about our response. Tell the person asking that you'd like to think about it. A "yes" speaks for itself. A "no" need not have any qualifiers or excuses, and they are seldom required if you give your answer after what I call "a cooling down for consideration" time period. As the old adage goes: " 'No' is a complete sentence!"

Take your lunch or dinner break. You earned it. Use the time to take a walk outside, have a cup of coffee, or catch up with friends. Pack or purchase a healthy meal and eat it *away from your desk and out of your office.*

Set goals

Keep a work journal and write down your goals. Expand on them as you go along. Note achievements and what remains to be done. Write down what you will need in terms of time, effort, education, and so on to achieve those goals, which can be as minor or as grandiose as you please. *They are yours.*

Focus on solving problems or issues instead of just venting. Venting is helpful, but has its limitations. It burdens other people who may not be experiencing the same thing, and at the same time allows you to brood about your problems and irritations, often magnifying them. If you must vent, vent to someone you know to be trustworthy and who will respect your confidence. Using a reflective journal can also help in figuring out responses to issues as well as how to solve them.

Focus on what is ahead of you, not behind you. We are all prone to ruminating over past failures: things we said that we shouldn't have, things we failed to see, things we saw and did nothing about. It's done. Over. Mourn fast and move on. Dwelling on past failures or grievances deprives you of precious time in the present and clouds your view of the future. Don't fall prey to that kind of thinking.

Focus on your strengths. You have many of them! If it helps, list your good qualities. Write down instances in which you achieved something that made you proud of yourself. You did it before; you can and will do it again.

Seek and Maintain Connections

Set up a support system for yourself, both within and without your organization. Have a go-to person whom you trust and get along well with.

Consider seeking a mentor who can guide you along professionally. So many of us suffer from a lack of confidence, especially when we are run down. A mentor can help in so many ways. Mine always tells me that good times don't last, but bad times don't either.

Don't be afraid to ask for advice! Far too many of us struggle alone. It is unnecessary and damaging to our sense of self.

Maintain contact with friends and family on a regular basis. Proximity to and connection with others go a long way in keeping us mentally and physically healthy. When I don't have time or energy in a particular day or week for face-to-face contact, I will make quick phone calls just to touch base or send a quick text to let people know I am thinking about them. If you don't have time in a particular week to meet someone for dinner or coffee, make plans for sometime in the future. It will maintain that connection while at the same time giving you something to look forward to!

FINAL THOUGHTS

I chose the epigraph for this chapter carefully for a good reason: it is often seen as an act of selfishness or self-indulgence to take care of one's self. Nothing could be further from the truth. We can deplete ourselves to the point of utter and complete emptiness, and then find ourselves paralyzed by our limitations. Better to get into the habit of caring for ourselves so that in turn we can care for others. I am grateful every day to work in an absolutely wonderful profession.

Most of us begin to care for ourselves holistically because we can no longer function in the old way. According to David Whyte, "A life's work is not a series of stepping-stones onto which we calmly place our feet, but more like an ocean crossing where there is no path, only a heading, a direction, which, of itself, is in conversation with the elements." We can't always know what the elements will throw at us, but we can change our response to it, which should keep us indispensable for a long time![1]

NOTE

1. David Whyte, *Crossing the Unknown Sea: Work as a Pilgrimage of Identity* (New York: Riverhead Books, 2002).

Index